Networking

I0504917

Coffee not Cocktails

Janet Shaner

© 2019 Janet Shaner

ISBN: 978-0-359-68275-1

All rights reserved, including the right to reproduce this book, or portions thereof in any form. No part of this text may be reproduced, transmitted, downloaded, decompiled, reverse engineered, or stored, in any form or introduced into any information storage and retrieval system, in any form or by any means, whether electronic or mechanical without the express written permission of the author.

Published by Top10 Learning Solutions Sàrl. Lausanne, Switzerland.

Table of Contents

Acknowledgments

As with most good things in life, this book has been enhanced through the collaboration and help of people in my network.

Critiques on different stages of drafts and ideas to make it more interesting and accessible came especially from Kevin Anselmo, Mope Ogunsulire and Andreas Wettstein.

Lindsay McTeague edited with her usual eagle eye and constructive suggestions, and she provided the inspiration for the cover design. Fiona Cook also shared her creative insights.

Special thanks go to those who shared their real world networking wisdom: Andreas, Barbara, Benedikt, Bryan, Grady, Harshul, Jordi, Kevin, Louisa, Mika, Nathalie, Nora, Olivier, Pat, Paul, Peggy, Peter, Ruud, Tomas and Tomoko. Some names have been disguised, but their stories are real.

Thanks also to those who generously agreed to have their research included. While the task of asking for permission was at first daunting, it turned out to be one of the most interesting parts of the project and led to some new connections.

And finally, thanks to those who have supported me during the highs and lows of writing this book: my family, my Scots Kirk friends, Suzanne Godfrey and Rusty.

Introduction

Most of us understand that networking is important in business and in many other facets of our lives. A good network can help you to obtain new ideas, access resources, raise funds, gain clients, build your reputation, find a better job, get promoted and more. Networking is often perceived as meeting new people through events and taking as much as possible. Research, however, suggests something different.

The science behind networking shows that there is a relationship between your network and performance when the right combination of *people*, *types of relationships* and *level of connectedness* is aligned with your objectives and context. This book connects the research with practical applications and real-world experiences of executives to help you create a networking strategy that is right for *you*.

Networking is defined by different dictionaries as:

- "The process of trying to meet new people who might be useful to you in your job, often through social activities."[1]

- "The exchange of information or services among individuals, groups, or institutions."[2]

- "The process of meeting and talking to a lot of people, especially in order to get information that can help you."[3]

- "Creating a group of acquaintances and associates and keeping it active through regular communication for mutual benefit.[4]

These definitions imply that networking is about building relationships. Networking science says that we build relationships with people who are similar to us, are located near us and with whom we have shared activities. It suggests that networking is more about coffee and less about cocktails. More about being involved with activities and less about networking events. More about building relationships and less about collecting business cards. More about giving and less about taking.

I find this hugely exciting.

It means that you don't have to attend every event imaginable to build a good network. Instead, you can do this over coffee, in smaller group settings or by participating together in work or other activities. If you enjoy group events, this is fine. But as we shall see later, the research suggests that relationships are built over time and through shared experiences, so you need to be doing things with others to develop meaningful relationships. Furthermore, there are different ways to build a network, and the "best" approach depends on your objectives and situation. This book will help you understand the different possibilities.

My interest in networks: The science is different from the stereotype

I learned about the science of social networks when I read the research as the foundation for a new course we were developing in an MBA program. This research suggests that networks are built with a wide range of people, including colleagues, clients, suppliers, university classmates, neighbors, family, friends, etc. Relationships with these people can be strong or weak, and the people can be connected to each other in different patterns. Depending on your situation and current objective, each of these patterns can constitute a "good" network. It is much more complex than just meeting new people. Relationships are built because we do something meaningful together, not because we attend a single event and then connect on LinkedIn.

I thought this was interesting because it was so different from the networking stereotype. If managers could understand this wider range of networking approaches, they could be more effective in their efforts. The relationship between business networks and profitability in a multinational company was the subject of my doctoral thesis, and I continue to read the research and relate it to real-world practice and the performance of practicing managers.

A few years ago, I became an entrepreneur, and the importance of my network was reinforced. According to the research, most of your business as an entrepreneur comes from your network – either people you know or through referrals – and I have found this to be true. And networking as an entrepreneur is different from networking in an organization. Understanding these differences has helped me to develop a more effective networking strategy for my new situation. This book can help you do this too.

Book structure: Theory, applications, techniques and analysis

This book is different because it builds on research to provide guidance on how to build a *networking strategy* and *plan*. Most networking books focus on the tactics of how to meet people and build relationships. This book is designed to provide an "end-to-end" solution, combining strategy and tactics for better results. Each chapter contains a section based on published networks research, practical applications, and stories from experienced executives to illustrate how this research is applied in practice. If your instinctive reaction is to cringe at the idea of research, don't be put off. I have tried to distill it to the most interesting and relevant parts. All of the references are included at the back of the book, so if you find a particular topic interesting, I encourage you to explore the original in more depth.

The book is divided into four parts:

- *Research foundations*: This explains the theory behind how we build relationships (the art) and what types of networks to build (the science). In terms of the art, people build relationships based on self-similarity, proximity and shared activities; energizing and giving are important behaviors for effective networks; and people have different networking styles. In terms of the science, networks have different structures based on the characteristics of the people, the strength of their ties and how they are connected to each other. Each of these elements relates to performance depending on the individual situation.

- *Specific applications*: There are detailed studies on networks in relation to entrepreneurs; women, minorities and expats; job search; and organizations. The research provides guidance on how to build an effective network in each of these situations.

- *Networking tools and techniques*: Events and technology play a role in building your network. These chapters explain how and why. They give advice on meeting new people, following up over coffee and staying in touch using technology.

- *Network analysis and action plan*: Here you will find step-by-step directions to chart and analyze your network to suit your situation and objectives. This is followed by guidance on how to develop a plan to enhance your network for better results.

Although the research may seem to present situations "in black and white," and applied to specific contexts, try to keep an open mind. Consider each chapter as a guide to help you understand the nuances of networks so you can apply them to your own situation in a more sophisticated and effective way.

Reading this book: Start where you like

The book has been designed so you can start reading the section most appealing or relevant to you. If you are someone who likes to understand the theory first, start there and then drill down to see how it applies to the specific applications. If you are interested in a specific application, for example if you are an entrepreneur, or a woman/minority/expat, or looking for a job, read that chapter and work backwards to the theory related to your case. Or you may want to start by drawing the picture of your network in Chapter 9 and then go back to explore how it relates to the theory and your context. Wherever you start, I suggest that you try some of the questions and examples and reflect on how your network fits with your situation and objectives. Then refer back to the science to see what specific changes you could make to create a more effective network and achieve better results. As the executive in one story says, you don't have to make all of the changes at once. Start small and build toward the network you want to achieve.

Real stories: Evolution of networking over a career

Throughout this book, I have included stories from real people, i.e. executives in my network, to illustrate the points. The goal is to help you see that these research ideas really do apply in practice. As a warm-up, read these stories describing executives' approach to networking and how it has changed over their career.

Mika

At the start of my career I thought networking meant going to a cocktail party. Now I understand it is about creating a meaningful relationship – quality vs. quantity. It is not just your number of LinkedIn connections or the business cards you collect. Young people worry that they have nothing to offer. In my experience, you can always bring value. Perhaps not in the immediate moment, but in the meeting follow-up. You can forward an article about a topic discussed or find another way to help and create a connection.

Andreas

My approach to networking has become more relaxed over the years. In the past I saw networking as meeting people at events. Today I see it as building meaningful and energizing relationships, which then may lead to business opportunities, but don't necessarily have to.

Pat

I continue to work to nurture connections with everyone I work with. If you stay in an industry, no one ever goes away, they just change companies. Having a reputation within the network of being someone who does high quality work and is truly a team player is huge. I understand how critical it is to have the right approach, and today I am more comfortable just telling people the help I'd like. Right now I want to add a new client. I have complete comfort reaching out to people, telling them my goal and asking for their ideas. We are a mutual aid society. They know I will be there for them whenever help is needed.

Benedikt

Networking reminds me of what I concluded about raising children; it's not what you do now that has a real impact, it's what you did five years ago that really influences what's happening now. Project this into the future, and you will realize that what you do now will have little impact on today's situation, but will have an impact five years down the road somehow.

Tomoko

At the start of my career, I didn't understand the concept of networking and didn't understand its value. There is a certain single-minded attitude at the start of a career that if one works hard and works well, one will be recognized and rewarded. Nowadays, I see networking as a sharing of experiences and, increasingly, as a source of information exchange. I enjoy meeting new people, hearing their stories and learning about things. As a part-time entrepreneur, I don't have the luxury of time to become an expert at things that could help move my business. So I seek out new connections so I can do some targeted and purposeful information gathering and sharing.

Grady

My approach to networking has changed over my career in that before I looked for "like-minded people." Now I just look for people. I am much more open. It is great fun, I have learned a lot and it has expanded my horizons.

Summary

Anyone can be good at building relationships and thus their network. You just need to have the right attitude, strategy and plan. A good network can help you, for example, to obtain new ideas, access resources, raise funds, gain clients, build your reputation, find a better job and get promoted. Effective networks have the right people, types of relationships and level of connectedness aligned with your unique objectives and situation.

If you consider yourself a "natural networker," you may know all of these things instinctively – and if this is the case, bravo. You can still learn about the different networking styles and approaches to help you be more effective in your own situation. Typically, people are good at one or a few approaches instead of the full range. Perhaps your style works well for meeting new people and gathering new ideas. If your objective is to transfer these ideas to your organization, you may achieve better results by partnering with someone talented at building close and trusting relationships.

If, however, networking is not easy for you, do not despair. If you are able to connect it with a purpose that is deeply meaningful, you might find that you learn how to do it better and even enjoy it. This book is designed to help you link research and practice to be more confident in building your network and create a networking strategy that is right for you.

Part 1: Research Foundations

The first part of this book describes the theory underpinning networks. It includes the art of networking or how we build relationships, followed by the science of networking or what types of relationships to build.

Key concepts you will learn are:

The art of networking: How we build relationships

- Self-similarity, proximity and shared activities are the three key principles guiding who we choose to build relationships with.

- Energizers are four times more likely to be effective networkers.

- Givers with boundaries are better networkers, and people perceived as innovators are those who both help often and request help often.

- People have different networking styles: Kingpin seeking, matchmaking, access and amiability.

The science of networking: What types of relationships to build

- Networks are built on three elements: The people in the network (composition), the strength of the relationship between them (tie strength) and the way they are connected to each other (structure).

- Each of these elements relates to different measures of performance depending on your situation and objectives.

- Networks may evolve over the life cycle of your idea or project.

1

The art of networking: Building relationships

Overview

The art of networking is building relationships. The people in your network come from all of your life experiences: work relationships, former classmates, family and friends, and extracurricular activities. Each of these groups can contribute to your efforts, depending on what you are trying to achieve. Your attitude and approach to giving and receiving makes a difference, and if you have been an energizer in these relationships you are four times more likely to be a good networker. In addition, we all have different networking styles, and recognizing your style will help you to enhance your networking efforts. Finally, it takes time to build and deepen your relationships, and you need to make an effort to do this if you want to sustain them.

Heidi Roizen: The importance of networks over a career[5]

In a famous Harvard Business School case study, entrepreneur Heidi Roizen describes the importance of networks and networking over her career: first as an entrepreneur, then as head of partner relationships with Apple and finally as a venture capitalist. Heidi emphasizes that networking is about building relationships with different types of contacts – people she finds interesting and smart, including a mix of personal and professional contacts – and making connections between people in her network only if it is win-win for both parties.

Heidi's networking approach includes managing the number of times each year she asks someone for a favor; the busier the person, the fewer times she asks. In addition, she uses an attitude of reciprocity, trying to create a balance of give and take in every relationship. Finally, referrals are an important element in her approach, and she often helps others by referring them to companies where she believes there might be a fit.

Heidi summarizes her approach to networking as having access to people and developing relationships over time, responding and helping, doing what you promise, balancing giving and receiving, and being consistent in each interaction.

The research

Developing a network means forming relationships with people. While some may be better at it than others, anyone can learn, especially if you understand how it works.

Building relationships: Self-similarity, proximity, shared activities

We establish relationships with people following three principles that identify different ways we have things in common with others. [6]

- **Self-similarity principle**: We build relationships with people who are similar to us in terms of training, experience, looks, politics, etc.

- **Proximity principle**: We build relationships with people with whom we spend the most time, for example at work in the office next door or on the same floor, our neighbors, people we see every day on the bus, in business incubators, etc.

- **Shared activities principle**: Potent networks are forged through shared activities that evoke passion, require interdependence and offer risk and reward. For example, classmates following the same tough program, participants on intense team-building activities or team mates in a sports club.

Energizers: Four times more likely to be effective networkers

Your attitude is another important element in building relationships, and one aspect is your level of energy creation. People identified as *energizers* are four times more likely to be effective networkers because they build foundations of trust and have constructive interactions with others (see *Table 1*).[7]

Table 1. Characteristics of energizers

Build foundations of trust	**Have constructive interactions with others**
• Create personal connections	• Engage in possibilities
• Build reciprocity	• Stay attentive in meetings
• Follow through on commitments	• Help others contribute to meetings and other activities
• Stand for something larger than themselves	• Disagree productively
	• Are flexible

Source: Cross, Baker and Parker (2003)[7]

People can also be perceived as *de-energizers* or people who "suck the life" out of the room. More specifically, they are described as:

> *People who have an uncanny ability to drain the life out of a group. These energy-sappers are avoided wherever possible, even when they have expertise to contribute in solving a problem. When a meeting with a "de-energizer" is unavoidable, people often waste time dreading it and mentally rehearse how they will cope. ... Thus de-energizers not only drain the people they meet but often affect the productivity of people they might not even know.[8]*

These de-energizers do not build trust and, in fact, may create distrust and reduce the productivity of the organization. Over the long term, they are not effective at building networks.

Some examples of energizing and de-energizing behaviors that come to mind are shown in *Table 2*.

Table 2. Energizing vs. de-energizing behaviors

Energizing behaviors	De-energizing behaviors
Responding in a timely manner to emails, even if the answer to a question or opportunity is "no thank you."	**Seldom responding** to emails, often requiring the sender to follow up with a phone call or in person visit in order to get an answer.
Being on time and prepared for meetings. Being flexible when someone needs to change a meeting time (when it is possible).	**Coming late, leaving early or even not attending** meetings. Frequently changing meeting times for the benefit of oneself vs. the team.
Giving feedback in a constructive way and with concrete suggestions about how to make something better.	Giving **feedback centered on identifying problems** without providing constructive solutions.
Participating in brainstorming groups to **generate ideas** about how things could be changed or enhanced – and being willing to help with the implementation.	Playing the role of a victim by **not taking responsibility** for actions and outcomes.
Showing genuine concern for others in a group, for example, by expressing support in times of challenge and sharing excitement when things go well.	**Not recognizing** the contributions of others.
Making time to do things together, for example, having lunch or coffee, participating in shared activities or attending events in support of others.	

The actions required to be an energizer are not difficult, i.e. being constructive, following through, listening and being positive. It does, however, take time and energy to consider the needs of others in addition to your own. This investment pays off significantly in the trust you build and increased ability to get things done.

Give and take: The importance of reciprocity

According to Adam Grant, professor and organizational psychologist at Wharton, people can be classified as givers, takers or matchers in the way they share in relationships. Givers are willing to help others either with their own resources or by opening their network with no expectation of something in return or with an expectation that the person will "pay it forward" by helping someone else in the future. Matchers have a "tit for tat" approach, meaning they expect something in return for the help they give, and they tend to keep score. If they help you with something, in the next exchange, you are expected to return the favor. Takers are all about what they can get for themselves. Grant suggests that the best networkers are "givers with boundaries."[9] These are people who, for example, define times to do their own work as well as to help others or people who help in small chunks such as making an introduction or giving a little feedback. They give without going overboard.

In addition, the combination of giving and receiving is crucial for value creation. As shown in *Figure 1*, those who both help often and request help often are the innovators, producers and value creators in an organization.[10]

One way to encourage a giving culture is to organize a "Reciprocity Ring." In this approach, people identify the help or information they need, either in a face-to-face encounter or in a group supported by technology. Group members provide suggestions of people or ideas that might help others achieve their goals. Systematizing this act of reciprocity helps to create a giving culture in an organization and enhance its ability to create stronger relationships and trust. Organizations also can use Givitas, a technology that allows the principles at work in the Reciprocity Ring to be applied every day.[11]

Figure 1. Innovators: Those who help often and request help often

	Request seldom	Request often
Help often	*Givers* Well-regarded, less productive	***Innovators,*** ***producers, value*** ***creators*** **Well-regarded,** **productive**
Help seldom	*Isolates* Least productive	*Takers* Less productive

Source: Baker (2016)[10]

Networking styles: Kingpin seeking, matchmaking, access, amiability

People have different styles in the way they build relationships. These have been described as kingpin seeking, matchmaking, access and amiability.[12] And of course there are strengths and weaknesses related to each style.

Kingpin seekers develop a network of relationships with people who can keep them informed about what is happening in an organization and who is most influential in the decision making. They are sensitive to the quality of information and the accuracy of interpretation of events. This capability is especially appropriate for gathering information in uncertain situations, obtaining different interpretations of ambiguous events, identifying how power is distributed and understanding who are the key decision makers and their perspectives and concerns.

Regina is a good example of a kingpin seeker. She is well connected and tries to link with the top people in the organization and those who can help to achieve her objectives. During periods of reorganization, she aligns herself with those in power to stay on top of information and decision making. In client organizations, she knows key people and understands how the client ticks. With this wealth of information, she is able to develop products that align with client needs and to get the buy-in of those inside her own company. With her wealth of relationships, ability to gather information and ability to adapt, she survives wave after wave of organizational change, always coming out in a solid and performing position. Kingpin seekers tend to be more effective than others at influencing upward and across organizations, obtaining favorable decisions and getting tasks done effectively and efficiently.

Matchmakers have excellent skills in connecting people, for example by creating activities where people can meet to share ideas, and linking people who have complementary needs. Matchmaking is especially suited to seeing the possibility of mutual interests and common ground between unfamiliar parties, building deeper relationships between different parts of the organization and sparking creative outcomes from two parties that typically do not interact. Matchmakers actively try to bridge gaps in organizations and believe in the concept of reciprocity – giving and receiving.

Timothy is a great example of a matchmaker. He always comes to group events with a smile and positive energy. He makes an effort to meet everyone at the event, and if they mention a need, he tries to identify someone who could help. He introduces them if they are in the same room or connects them via email soon after he goes home. He is known as someone who can bridge different groups and bring them together for mutual benefit. The help Timothy gives is appreciated, so when he needs help, people are happy to give it in return. Matchmakers tend to be more effective at coordinating cross-department and cross-organizational tasks, obtaining access to information, ideas and resources not available through normal channels, creating synergy and deepening connections.

Having an *access* approach to networking means striving to build large and diverse networks and working to stay in touch with everyone. This style aligns with the stereotypical characterization of a "networker." Having an access approach helps with connecting large and diverse audiences, spending "face time" interacting with customers and business partners, and demonstrating trustworthiness, candor and openness to information.

Morgana is a good example of an access networker. She is involved in a wide range of organizations and activities, both personal and professional, and is always interested in meeting new people and helping them with their objectives. She actively stays in touch with people through email and face-to-face meetings, and her Christmas letter is famous for its creativity and the number of people to whom it is sent. Having an access style is beneficial for strengthening the quality of decisions based on accurate data and information, gathering information from the "front lines" and enhancing your public reputation as a leader.

Finally, those with an *amiability* style give others the impression that they always have time to listen and help. They try to create a positive atmosphere and avoid expressing negative feelings. They watch body language and listen to the context in which the message is delivered. This approach encourages the sharing of sensitive information, helping them learn more from their interactions with others. They tend to be central in an organization's informal friendship network.

Richard is a good example of someone with an amiability style. He has an amazing ability to connect quickly with people inside and outside the organization, and they often are willing to share sensitive personal information. He knows what is happening in the organization and has an instinctive sense when something isn't working, especially on the level of relationships. Having an amiability style helps in sharing sensitive and personal information, strengthening morale and increasing the number of people that turn to you for support in stressful or sensitive times.

As described above, we all have different networking styles, or perhaps no style at all. The research found that only 25% of those surveyed had one networking capability and only 2% had all four types of networking capabilities.[13]

Practical implications

How you approach your relationships makes a significant difference in your networking effectiveness. If you come to work or any other group activity with positive energy and a supportive attitude, people are more likely to trust you and want to work with you. Givers with boundaries and those who ask for help are also better networkers and innovators. The good news is that your attitude is within your control. Consider a few steps that you could take in this direction. For example, responding to emails promptly, being on time and prepared for meetings, giving constructive feedback and making time to get to know people better over lunch or coffee. These behaviors are relatively easy if you put your mind to it, and they will pay significant dividends in your relationships and trust with others.

In addition, building relationships requires spending time together on shared activities. It takes about 50 hours of socializing to go from acquaintance to casual friend, an additional 40 hours to become a "real" friend, and a total of 200 hours to become a close friend.[14] This may not sound like much time – a week or a month of work. But when you consider that, as adults, most of us already have jobs, families and other activities, finding time to build new relationships is a challenge.

Consider the math. If you belong to a professional networking group and want to get to know people better, you need to put in 50 hours with a few of the members. This equates to attending 25 2-hour events, joining a committee or participating in longer group activities. You need to find a very active group to achieve this within a year.

If you want to deepen your relationships with friends, you need to spend an additional 40 hours together, including more intense experiences. This could involve a long weekend away (2 days x 16 hours together = 32 hours) or monthly dinner or activity events (12 x 4 hours = 48 hours) to strengthen the relationship.

Finally, if you want to achieve the 200 hours to build close friends, you really need to make a commitment to spending time together, potentially through a range of activities. Something like coffee once a week (52 x 1 hours = 52 hours), dinner or a cultural activity once a month (12 x 4 hours = 48 hours), a day of walking, skiing or cycling once a month (12 x 8 hours = 96 hours). This combination would just get you to 200 hours over the course of a year. Of course, you don't have to achieve this in 12 months, but it is good to have some targets in mind.

Paul: Give as well as take makes the network stronger

When I was young, my approach to networking was selfish and self-focused. Networks were for exploiting to my advantage. I now see that networks are of great importance for a wider purpose. When I give as well as take it makes the network stronger and more effective. I get a greater sense of reward from being in a network. I learn more and am a better person, as I take less now because I see that there is not necessarily any benefit for me. Networks are dynamic. Mine has evolved due to changes related to my geographical location, my career, my personality and my values.

Nathalie: Giving pays benefits two years later

I knew John from many years ago in a different role. He came to London looking for a new career opportunity. Coincidentally, I happened to spot him at an event. I made a point of having a real discussion with him and walked away feeling like I fully understood what he was looking for. A few weeks later, I was invited to a closed event where many of the attendees could be helpful for John. I invited him to attend as my guest, made a few introductions and left the rest to him. A few months later I discovered he had landed a C-suite role.

Fast-forward two years. I received an email from John asking me to contact the head of Learning and Development in his company as they were looking for an Executive Coach for their leadership team. When I contacted his colleague, she mentioned that she already had a contact, however John had sung my praises and insisted that she speak to me. John made the introduction, and the rest was up to me…exactly what I had done for him!

Mika: An old connection becomes an acquisition partner, 30 years later

One story coming full circle is with a former customer in Australia that I used to call on early in my career. We struck up a friendship. I left the company in 1999, but we kept in touch via email and eventually Facebook. Two years ago, he became global chief medical officer for a large medtech company. When his company decided to acquire my California-based startup, he was one of the strongest supporters pounding on the table urging the CEO to do the deal. We celebrated working together again a few months ago in Boston!

Summary

The art of networking is building relationships with people. You build relationships with people who are similar to you, located close to you and with whom you have shared experiences. Being an energizer makes you four times more likely to be an effective networker, as does having an attitude of giving and reciprocity. If you want to build relationships and thus your network, you need to be sincerely interested and invest time through a range of activities to get to know people better, all building on your own networking style.

Questions for consideration

- *How did you get to know the people in your network?* Are they work colleagues, former classmates, neighbors or people similar to you?

- *Do you build energy in your relationships?* How could you change your behavior to enhance these capabilities?

- *What is your networking style:* Kingpin maker, matchmaker, access or amiability? Would it be helpful for you to develop another style?

- *How can you apply the art of networking to enhance your relationships?* What activities can you engage in to build new relationships or deepen existing ones? When should you consider building relationships over coffee and when by participating in larger events?

2

The science of networking: Aligning structure with objectives

Overview

Networks are built on three elements:

1. The people in the network (*composition*)

2. The strength of the relationships between them (*tie strength*)

3. How they are connected to each other (*structure*)

Each of these elements has a relationship with positive outcomes in different ways. For example, the composition of your network should be aligned with your objective. The strength of your network ties should be aligned with the type of information you need to share. And the structure of your network should be aligned with your context or environment. Finally, your network may evolve over the life cycle of your idea or project. If you can understand how these variables relate to each other, you can create a network that is right for you and your situation.

Janet: Networking strategy building on science

While I was helping to create a new course for an MBA program, a colleague suggested that I explore research on social networks to understand its foundations. With this fortuitous introduction, I learned more and found it fascinating. Before this, I had thought that networking was only about the stereotypical "access" approach of handing out business cards and frequenting cocktail parties. In contrast, the research suggested a much wider variety of approaches and structures that were more or less effective depending on the situation.

I thought if someone could learn more about these differences and when to apply them, he or she could develop a more strategic approach to networking that would relate to better outcomes. This was the theme of my doctoral research, and my idea was confirmed in the context of one multinational company.

Since launching my own company, the importance of networking has been reinforced. Most business comes either from direct contacts or referrals, and I am constantly reconnecting with people in my network whom I have gotten to know over a period of many years. I really enjoy meeting them for coffee or catching up over Skype. Sometimes these conversations relate to business. Other times they are just about reconnecting. Either way, it is a pleasure to stay connected and to discuss ideas for mutual benefit.

The research

Social network analysis provides the tools for graphing and measuring networks.[15] It includes three elements as part of an individual's network (see *Figure 2*):

- *People (composition)*: The type of people in your network or "who" – the different shapes.

- *Relationship (tie strength)*: The types of relationships between your contacts or how close they feel to each other, referred to as strong or weak ties – the thickness of the lines.

- *Connectedness (structure)*: How the people in your network are connected to each other – the graph.

There is no "best" network structure. Instead, your network should fit with your objectives, your environment and the type of information that you need to share. The next sections discuss these different contingencies.

Figure 2. The elements of a network

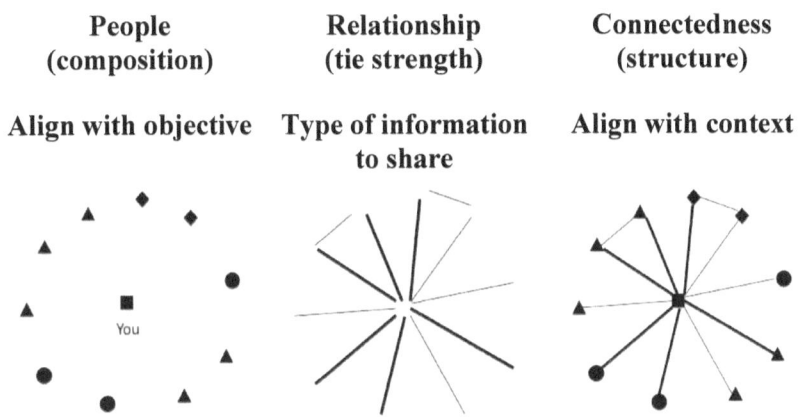

People (composition)	Relationship (tie strength)	Connectedness (structure)
Align with objective	Type of information to share	Align with context

People in the network: Aligned with your objective

Often we relate networking to meeting as many new people as possible. In many situations, this is not the most effective approach. First, it takes a huge amount of time. Second, research shows it's not about having just anyone in your network – the key is having the *right* people.

The composition of your network relates to your objective. If you need to gather new information, having a diverse set of contact types is helpful to assemble a wide range of ideas. In contrast, if your objective is the profitability of your organization or client base, having a majority of customers and suppliers in your network will give you the best outcome because it relates to generating revenue or reducing costs. As examples, in an inspection service company, external business networks with a high proportion of customers and suppliers related significantly to profitability. [16] For biotech startups, having contacts with pharmaceutical companies, universities, government laboratories, and research institutes related positively to performance measures including patenting and revenue growth, while industry association contacts related negatively to revenue growth.[17] Links with venture capitalists and universities also made a difference.[18]

Relationship strength: Depends on the type of information you need to share

Relationship ties are classified as *strong* or *weak* depending on your perception of the strength of the relationship. People we have known for less time or with whom we feel "less close" are classified as *weak ties*. We have *strong ties* with people we have known for a long time or with whom we feel "close."[19] Relationships are built over time and, as described in Chapter 1, it takes about 50 hours of socializing to go from acquaintance to casual friend, an additional 40 hours to become a "real" friend, and a total of 200 hours to become a close friend.[20] Relationship strength also can be measured by how close you feel to a person, perhaps because you share similar characteristics and interests and can develop a trusting relationship more easily – even if you have spent less time with them.

Weak ties are best for transferring explicit knowledge or facts, and these ties can help in the search for innovation or finding a job. These relationships take less effort to maintain, so you are likely to have weak ties with a wider range of people.[21] Examples of weak ties are acquaintances such as neighbors, people you have met in professional organizations or work colleagues outside your direct team.

In contrast, *strong ties* are those where you feel closer to people and perhaps have a relationship with them on multiple levels, for example work colleagues who are also friends, fellow board members in organizations to which you belong, or close family and friends. Strong ties are essential for transferring tacit knowledge (skills, ideas or experiences that may be difficult to express), complex ideas and proprietary information because this requires trust.[22] Feeling close to someone is a signal that you have confidence that sensitive information will remain confidential.

Kevin: Weak ties for business development

I founded a small communications consulting company five years ago. It has been interesting to see how loose connections have been helpful in pointing me in the right direction for work. I always felt that individuals I worked with directly would be my biggest fans. In actuality, it has been connections that I didn't perceive to be strong that have been most helpful.

In one case, a former colleague who I perhaps collaborated with on just a very small number of projects made a crucial introduction that led to a project that lasted almost two years. In another scenario, an individual who I knew only virtually as the result of a common interest in podcasting introduced me to someone that led to a new project. In another instance, a former colleague who I actually didn't get along with so well was instrumental in bringing me on for a client project once she had transitioned to a new role. All three scenarios have led to work assignments that I enjoyed professionally and also enable me to continue running my business from a financial point of view.

Network structure: Open, connected, sponsor or mixed depending on your context

Network structures can be described as open, connected, sponsor or mixed based on the number of interconnections between the people (see *Figure 3*).

In *open networks*, few people are connected to each other. They are good for gathering information because each member provides access to different types of information that is not mutually shared. Open networks also provide opportunities for brokerage and power because the person in the middle controls the information flow.

Connected networks provide safety and security because everyone shares similar information and if one member betrays the group, he or she is ostracized, making this action risky.

Sponsor networks are those in which one member is also connected to many others and may be the person who introduced you to the network. Sponsor networks are good for referrals or new situations where one person can benefit from the established connections and reputation of another.[23]

As the name suggests, *mixed networks* combine the benefits of open and connected networks, for example to gain access to a wide range of information from one part of the network and then share it with another more closely connected group in the network.[24]

Figure 3. Types of network structures

Open: Gather information

Connected: Safety and security

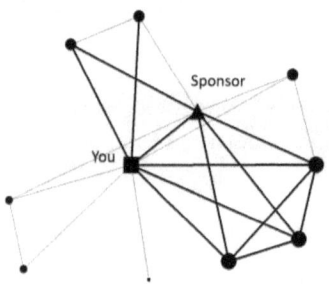

Sponsor: Reputation and referral

Mixed: Combine information and trust

Source: Burt (1998)[23], Uzzi (1999)[24]. Graphs created with UCINet. [68]

Network contingencies: Aligned with your situation

Each of the networks described above has strengths or weaknesses depending on your situation.

Knowledge search vs. knowledge transfer

If your goal is to gather new knowledge, open networks with weak ties work well, allowing you to reach new people and new sources of information outside of your normal exchanges. If your goal is knowledge transfer, then connected networks with strong ties help to facilitate the trust required to share explicit knowledge and complex ideas.[25]

Developing vs. mature industries

Different industries have different approaches to networking. In the constantly changing semiconductor industry, for example, open networks with weak ties provide the flexibility to *explore* new technologies and adjust to the ever-moving set of competitors and technologies. In the more mature steel industry, connected networks with strong ties facilitate the trust required to *exploit* technology and find process improvements to improve profitability.[26]

Certain vs. uncertain business environments

Different countries have different approaches to networks. Child psychology suggests that the first need of a person or an organization is safety and security.[27] In the business environment, this may be provided either by the legal system or, when that is inefficient, by a connected network. In countries where the legal environment functions relatively well (for example, northern Europe, North America or Australia), individuals or organizations can have open networks to gather information and facilitate innovation. In countries where the legal environment functions less efficiently (for example, southern Europe, Russia, China, Africa or Latin America), the first need of a network is to provide safety and security, and this is done through connected networks.[28] Some of these countries even have special names for relationship building, for example *guanxi* in China, *blat* in Russia and *pratik* in Haiti.[29]

Harshul: Differences between countries[30]

If I look at my experience in Singapore or Europe, the networks are much more closed. In Silicon Valley, even if I just met you, I would open up my network to you without any reservations, whereas in Asia or in Europe, it takes a while. There needs to be trust first, before the network is opened to you.

Tomas: Comparing Silicon Valley and China[31]

In America, it is much more transactional and you engage in a relationship with somebody initially if there is mutual benefit and things are very clear and very transparent. The relationship is more at face value. In China, when you engage in guanxi *building, you may have a specific objective in mind for developing that* guanxi, *but you never really know how it will turn out, and you still invest a lot of time. If somehow you succeed in building that relationship, in achieving your initial objective, chances are that you will achieve much more.*

Barbara: Networking in Italy through recommendations

When I worked in Italy, I found that people are often hired – especially in consulting relationships – on the strength of the network relationship as compared to the qualifications. As an American outside this culture, I would be recommended to run a training program for a company without being asked for any details about the course content. "I am sure that you are really good at what you do." I was trusted completely, based on the strength of the recommendation.

Established reputation vs. new

Network structure also relates to the reputation and legitimacy of a person or organization. If you have a well-established reputation or are considered "legitimate" in a situation, for example, you are established in a company and similar to others in the organization, then an open network facilitates access to information and power. If you are new to a situation and not yet considered legitimate, this open network approach may result in your being perceived as arrogant or pushy. In these circumstances, having a sponsor to recommend and refer you to others helps to smooth the transition and establish your credibility, building on the legitimacy of your sponsor.[32]

Combining the benefits

Mixed networks may combine the benefits of open and connected networks. For example, small businesses that maintained weak relationships with a larger number of banks combined with stronger relationships with a few principal lenders were able to scan the market for lower interest rates and innovations in financial services and then negotiate for similar advantages with the banks where they had close relationships and thus obtain a lower cost of capital.[33] Building on this idea of mixing information, the best returns were generated by investors

28

who drew ideas from a wide variety of other traders but did not follow the herd.[34]

As you can see, there are several contingency factors related to a network structure that is aligned with your objectives and context. These are summarized in *Table 3* and will be applied to specific situations in succeeding chapters.

Table 3. Contingencies and alignment with network elements

Contingency	Composition		Tie strength		Network structure			
	Similar	Diverse	Strong	Weak	Open	Connected	Sponsor	Mixed
Business goal:								
• New ideas		X						
• Profitability	X							
Information:								
• Gather new		X		X	X			
• Transfer existing			X			X		
Industry:								
• Growing				X	X			
• Mature			X			X		
Country environment:								
• Certain					X			
• Uncertain						X		
Reputation/ legitimacy								
• Established/ majority					X			
• New/minority							X	
Job search				X			X	
Innovation		X						X

Life cycle of an idea journey: Network structures over time

The life cycle of an idea journey illustrates how these network structures combine and evolve as the idea develops (see *Figure 4*). In the idea generation stage, where the involvement of contacts is passive and serendipity plays a key role, weak ties and open networks provide access to new ideas. As the idea progresses, connected networks with strong ties help to elaborate the idea in safety, and a sponsor can help to champion the idea in the market. When an idea reaches the implementation stage, mixed networks facilitate the combination of idea production in the safety of a connected network, with an open network reaching outside to sell the idea and make an impact on the market.[35]

Figure 4. Network evolution: Life cycle of an idea journey

	Generation	Elaboration	Championing	Implementation
Contacts' involvement	Indirect, passive			Direct, active
Creators' intentionality	Serendipitous			Intentional
Network type	Open, weak ties: New ideas	Connected, strong ties: Support	Sponsor, referral: Idea legitimacy	Mixed, Connected: Idea production Open: Idea impact

Source: Adapted from Perry-Smith and Mannucci (2017)[35]

Practical implications

Different network elements correlate with positive results depending on your objectives, the type of information you need to share, your industry and country environment, and your reputation and legitimacy position. To understand your network and how it fits with your situation, you can analyze it following the step-by-step approach described in Chapter 9. Once you have done this, you can identify actions to enhance your network.

If you need to open your network or build weak ties for exploration, you could talk more frequently to your peers, join new organizations, have lunch with different people at work, go to industry conferences, or use technology such as alumni directories or LinkedIn to identify people with similar characteristics as you.

If you need to build stronger relationships and a more connected network for security, try to build on common interests, establish trust and introduce people in your network who do not know each other. Good ways to deepen relationships are through shared projects or intense activities, getting to know people outside of work and making time to develop the relationship.

If you are new to an industry or country, think about how the networking approach you have learned may be similar or different to the new one. For example, a manager skilled in building networks in a more entrepreneurial environment (e.g. the United States or a young business) may need guidance to understand networking in a closed network environment (e.g. Russia or a mature business) and vice versa. For companies, learning and development professionals would do well to coach managers on how to adapt to their new situation if they do not already have the networking skills that fit.

If you need to establish credibility, try to identify others who are considered legitimate in the situation and strive for a referral. Identify people whom you know well and could introduce you to others, for example, former classmates, team members or colleagues. You can also start by joining clubs related to an activity where you already have legitimacy, for example join a sports club if you are an athlete or an expat organization if you have recently arrived in a country. You will meet people in these organizations with whom you will make a faster connection and who can then introduce you to others in their network.

Finally, consider the benefits of a mixed network, for example having an open network outside your organization to gather new ideas combined with a more connected network inside your organization to commercialize these ideas. Or perhaps a more open network during a period of change combined with a connected network of family and friends to support you through the challenging time.

Pat: Building relationships through shared experiences

I was so lucky in that the first company I joined after my MBA was a fantastic place that gave me the opportunity to develop deep connections with many high quality people. It was a startup and one of the things they did particularly well was to hire very good people. I worked there for 11 years before they were acquired by a large multinational. I stayed on for about 5 years, so it was a long time in total. Throughout those years, I developed incredible bonds with so many people. We went through formative phases of the company and subsequent transformative phases. Through it all the connections deepened.

After this, I spent a few years at another company and then began my own consulting company. Every bit of consulting work I have done has come from the connections developed in my first company. The team has gone on to populate many, many companies in this industry. They have given me the source of my livelihood and my professional fulfillment. More than that, they are a virtual community, always there and ready to lend a hand. They are good friends.

As I sit in my home office, I look out on a beautiful tree in my garden. It is about 20 feet tall and just lovely. A group of six friends gave me the tree when my mother passed away 17 years ago. I was too grief-stricken at the time to focus on the tree, other than appreciating their gesture. I asked my gardener to find a place for it. He planted it in my driveway where I pass it many times a day. Every time I see it, I am reminded of the kindness of my dear friends.

Summary

Networks have three key elements: people (composition), relationships (tie strength) and connectedness (structure). These can be graphed and measured. Each of these elements and combinations has strengths and weaknesses, and the best approach depends on your situation. The people in your network should be aligned with your objective. Strong or weak relationships should be aligned with the type of information you need to share. Your network structure should be aligned with your need to gather new information through an open network, to provide safety and security through a connected network, to establish reputation and legitimacy through a sponsor network or to combine these benefits through a mixed network. The key is to build a network aligned with your unique situation to achieve better results.

Questions for consideration

- *What is your objective related to your network*: New ideas, profitability, reputation building or support? Do you have contacts in your network who can contribute to these objectives?

- *What type of information do you need to share with your network?* Do you need to develop more weak ties to share facts or strong ties to share sensitive information?

- *How are your contacts connected to each other?* Do you have an open network for exploration? A connected network to provide safety and support? A sponsor network to refer you in new situations? Or a mixed network to combine the information gathering benefits of open networks with the support and trust in connected networks?

- *Is your network aligned with your situation?* What is the best approach for your industry or country environment or level of legitimacy? How could you adjust your network for better results?

Part 2: Specific Applications

The theory described in Part 1 is explored further here in four specific areas: entrepreneurs, women/minorities/expats, job search and organizational networks.

Key concepts you will learn are:

- *Entrepreneurs* need to gather information, identify investors, find employees, acquire customers and build their reputation. Having contacts who can help directly with this or who can make a referral to the right people relates most strongly with different measures of performance, including patenting, revenue growth and attracting employees.

- *Women, minorities and expats* need to establish their reputation, especially if they are among the minority in an organization. They need to build on the reputation of a sponsor for early career promotion and tend to have connections with people similar to them for support and friendship, and connections with the majority group for advice and influence.

- *Job seekers* rely on networks to access the hidden job market, which represents 60% of jobs. Weak ties are important sources of information, and referrals provide faster access to and credibility with a potential employer.

- *Organizational networks* are different from the organizational chart. Those more central in the network are more likely to facilitate change. Innovation is likely to come from mixed networks combining open networks and weak ties *outside* the organization for new ideas with connected networks and stronger ties *inside* the organization to commercialize these ideas.

3

Entrepreneurs: Accessing resources and building reputation

Overview

Entrepreneurs and startup companies feature prominently in the research, and their performance is related to having contacts who can facilitate access to needed resources and who can provide a referral to those with resources. Networks can help entrepreneurs to gather information, find employees, acquire customers, identify investors and build reputation. Startups typically have limited funds, so resources obtained through trusted networks are less costly, more targeted and more valuable. In addition, working with trusted and talented people as employees, customers and investors helps to minimize mistakes. The key objective for entrepreneurs is to build relationships with people aligned with their objectives

Bryan: The importance of a network for an entrepreneur

I am an entrepreneur, most recently as founder and CEO of a startup selling building energy management systems. Generally I like meeting new people and enjoy networking. In fact, one of my previous jobs was for a company that created a technology to enhance networking at large events.

In my current company, fundraising is one of my key objectives. So far, all of our funding has come through my network – either first or second level contacts. Investors are former colleagues, undergraduate and MBA classmates, and friends of friends or people referred to me through direct contacts. Former colleagues have invested the most because significant trust is built with someone when you work with them. It is also important to have a "tribe" circle, for example, from your university, a church or any organization of which you are a part. This group provides both resources and support critical in the startup phase, and the value of this circle depends on the strength of affiliation the members feel for your tribe.[36]

Over time, I have found that my second-degree contacts have been the most likely to invest. In searching for investors, I look for those who have connections to other investors, potential customers or prospective employees, in addition to financial resources. The network has also been a good source for employees because in a small company a hiring mistake can be costly, and an employee referred by someone already trusted has a greater chance of succeeding in the organization.

Now we are looking for the next round of funding to support rapid scale-up. I continue to leverage my network and that of our partners and investors to help us achieve this next level of growth.

The research

Bryan's approach ties in nicely with the research. Key elements for startup performance relate to building relationships with people who are potential customers, employees or investors or to access these resources through referrals by others, also building on their reputation.

In the case of biotech startups, relationships with pharmaceutical companies, universities, government laboratories, research institutes and marketing alliances were associated with different performance measures including patenting, revenue growth, employment, and research and development spending. Links with industry associations had a negative relationship with revenue growth.[37] The summary in *Table 4* shows that relationships with pharmaceutical companies had a positive relationship with performance across all categories because they could help the startup commercialize its product. If the company's objective was patenting and revenue growth, contacts with universities were also beneficial, potentially because they gave access to innovative ideas that translated into patents and revenue. Innovative ideas seemed more likely to come from universities than from research institutes. Research institutes were good sources of employees but they had no relationship with revenue growth.

37

Table 4. Biotech startup network composition and performance

Contact type	Patenting	Revenue growth	R&D employees	Non-R&D employees	R&D spending
Pharmaceutical company	+	+	+	+	+
University	+	+			
Government lab	+	-	+		+
Research institute			+	+	+
Marketing alliance		+	+	+	+
Industry association		-			-

Source: Baum, Calabrese and Silverman (2000) [37]

In other research, links to venture capitalists were associated with startup sales growth because venture capitalists who invested in a startup had an incentive to help the venture succeed, and they provided a strong positive signal to other investors. Startups' links to universities correlated with sales growth when combined with the internal capabilities to absorb the knowledge, and collaboration with universities and research institutes provided a means to develop technological knowledge that a startup could not do on its own. Startups that valued these resources were also better positioned to hire graduates and researchers through the ties.[38]

Gaining referrals through the network is critical for building the reputation of startups. For example, the reputation of the initial partners of new venture capital firms related positively to these firms' future status because established organizations were unlikely to risk their reputation by engaging in activities undesirable for future performance. Hence, partnering with a highly visible firm increased the newcomer's visibility and highlighted the newcomer as an attractive partner. Building on the reputation of an existing firm is a signal of quality, which is important especially in times of uncertainty.[39]

38

Practical implications

The key takeaway from this research is to understand where your company is in its life cycle and to cultivate relationships (directly or through referrals) with the types of contacts who can provide access to the resources needed at that stage, be they research ideas, customers, employees or funding. For example, technology startups may benefit from links with research universities, since locations near these universities or in innovation parks facilitate connections with new research and companies commercializing these ideas.

As you think about which customer segments to enter, you may want to prioritize those where you have the strongest network or the greatest potential for referrals. You may want to target potential customers and investors not only for their financial potential but also for their ability to help build your reputation quickly. Once you have identified the right types of people, find a way to make contact directly or ask someone to make an introduction and speed the connection process. Thinking back to Bryan's example, one of the criteria he used in looking for potential investors and partners was their ability to introduce him to building managers or architects who might buy the product or include it in their design specifications.

For referrals, identify "super-connectors" who are not themselves clients or investors, but who are connected to many of the types of people you need to meet. For example, investors who have invested previously in the industry of your target clients, event organizers who know all of the companies in your target industry, or a coach or consultant who offers complementary services to the same client base as yours. People buy from those they trust, so connections with credible people who can refer you through an introduction will build your reputation and make it easier to acquire future clients and investors.

Paul: Finding partners through serendipity

I had an idea to set up a specialized newspaper but had no experience in local media distribution and only a limited idea about how to approach it. Thinking who I might know with this experience, I realized that the husband of my wife's best friend was in the media distribution business. I contacted him to learn more. The idea seemed to have promise, but we lacked experience in financing startups. By serendipity, a mutual friend hosted a drinks party. One of the guests was standing on his own, so I approached him, and after chatting for a while, asked about his work. He replied, "I help small companies raise funds." The three of us together had all the core skills needed to launch the business idea, and it is still going today.

Tomoko: Building a network of entrepreneurs to understand their world

As I didn't have business colleagues and friends who were entrepreneurs, I had to expand my network. I started speaking to parents from my children's daycare and from the local public school. This was a group outside my existing business school alumni network. Here, I met quite a few entrepreneurs who shared their experiences with me.

A couple of years later, I decided to try my hand at a startup, and this network of entrepreneurs was able to provide more concrete information. I believe this happened once they understood that I was more serious about the endeavor. This network also helped by introducing me to other people and providing access to valuable information regarding funding possibilities and competitions. The more concrete my questions, the more concrete the recommendations I received.

Louisa: Finding clients through a fellow alumnus

I was networking with some former colleagues in the cable industry and one of them connected me to a cable and digital veteran. He connected me with a venture capital (VC) firm in New York specializing in tech and digital media. I met with a woman there who was in charge of, among other things, finding talent for portfolio companies. (I was looking for clients, not a full-time job.) She posted my bio on their internal site that their portfolio companies access.

A few months later I got an email from someone who went to my college saying he saw my name on this VC company's list and how it is unusual to see tech people like himself from our school. (We went to a small liberal arts college.) It turns out he was COO (now CEO) of a "content intelligence company." He suggested we meet for coffee, and we had a nice chat. We are not the same era, but we had a connection through the school. A year later he reached out to me to coach one of his executives, followed by another a year or so later. What really surprised me was that it was our alumni connection that made the difference. But I guess that is what networking is about.

Summary

Identifying clients for revenue generation, employees to translate vision into reality and investors for funding are key elements for startup success. Having people in your network who can help you access directly or refer you to these resources is the most critical networking element for entrepreneurs. To build an effective networking strategy, entrepreneurs should first identify their objectives and the types of contacts needed for the business to grow. They should also target funding partners who can provide not only financial resources but also access to potential customers and credibility in establishing the startup's reputation.

Questions for consideration

- *What resources does your company need?* Do you have the right types of contacts in your network that relate to your startup performance?

- *Who might you target for a referral?* Are there specific investors or well-known clients with whom you can work to build the company's reputation faster?

- *Where do you have a critical mass of contacts?* When you make choices about which markets to enter or customer segments to target, where do you have the greatest concentration of contacts for information or referral to help you build your business more quickly?

4

Women, minorities and expats: Different networks for support and for advice

Overview

While an open, access networking approach may be positive for the majority group or those considered "legitimate" in an organization, anyone who is part of a minority group (e.g. women, expats or a different racial group) faces a different story. In these cases, a sponsor is required to lend their reputation, provide access to advice and influence, and facilitate early promotion or other career-related benefits. In addition, the mix of people in the network differs. People in the majority group can have all of their needs met by others similar to them, whereas those in the minority group tend to have friendship and support networks with those similar to them, and advice and influence networks with people in the majority group.

Peggy: Doing a great job is not always enough

For many years I thought that if I did a great job at work, people would notice my skills and I would get promoted. It was only when I read the book Career GPS *by Ella L.J. Edmondson Bell that I realized that doing a great job, as a woman, is not always enough. You need to have people above your level recommending you for a promotion, a new project, etc. I also read Sheryl Sandberg's* Lean In, *and that was when I started putting myself in front of people, as I realized you need to speak to people to connect. I am shy by nature, so placing myself in front of a manager visiting from head office does not come easy to me. However, I have always been strong in facing my own fear and the more times you do it, the more natural it becomes. It is important, though, that it is not perceived as being pushy by the person you are trying to connect with.*

When I started my MBA, I asked my manager if the company had a mentor program, which it did. Now I have a mentor within the company who also took an MBA while working full time. However, he has a completely different job and sees things from a different angle. Halfway through my MBA, I started mentoring him in the soft skills and different angles on managing people. This type of networking has been a secure base. On a challenging assignment, he has been my sounding board for office politics, and the exposure I get internally from him speaking about me to other people is priceless.

The research

A common networking perception is that the best place to be is in the center of an open network because it gives the greatest access to information and power in connecting others. This position does in fact relate to performance as measured by early promotion, but only for those already considered legitimate in the organization – senior white men in the case of the study. In contrast, this approach led to the slowest promotion for those not considered legitimate, specifically women and those new in the organization. These groups first needed to establish credibility, and early promotion was associated with a network with a strong connection to a powerful, well-connected sponsor who could extend their legitimacy to the minority person in question (see *Figure 5*).[40]

Research in an advertising firm found that men built networks with other men for multiple purposes – communication, advice, support, influence and friendship – and these multiplex relationships created stronger ties between the men. In contrast, women built relationships with other women for social support and friendship, and relationships with men for advice and organizational support.[41] In this example, men represented the majority in the organization and the range of their professional relationship needs could be met by other men. For women, however, there were not enough women in certain positions to provide advice and organizational support, hence they had to diversify their networks to include the men who could provide access to those resources.

Figure 5. Network differences for majority vs. minority or those new in an organization

Majority group or established reputation: Open

Minority group or new in company: Sponsor

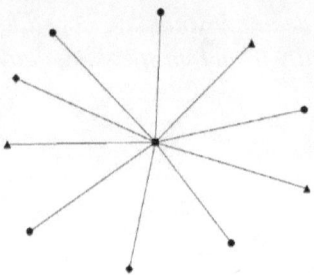
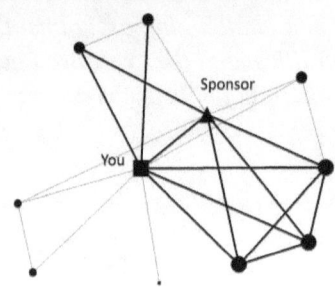

Source: Burt (1998)[40]

Similar network differences have been found between white men and minorities. For example, black managers developed advice, communication and influence relationships with white sponsors but did not rely on them for support that they could get more readily from other minorities,[42] a similar outcome to that described for women. As there were likely to be fewer black managers to provide advice and influence, they needed to diversify their networks to include white managers who had access to these resources.

In MBA classrooms, comparing the networks of men from the university's home country with women and international students showed similar patterns. Home country men built networks with each other, potentially missing out on the learning benefits that come from interacting with diverse classmates. Additionally, giving and receiving behavior was different such that giving help was associated with influence for home country men due to positive reputational effects, but it did not enhance the perceived influence of women, particularly among home country men.[43] Giving seemed to be an assumed characteristic of women, whereas men benefited from doing something supposedly out of character.

Practical implications

Those in the organizational minority who are not yet considered legitimate, such as women, expats and different racial groups, must initially develop networks built on the reputation of a sponsor in order to rise in the organization. Relationships with people similar to themselves provide friendship, social support and trust. Because there are fewer people like themselves in more senior positions, however, they must diversify their networks to include the majority group for resources such as advice and influence. This majority group, most often men, has the luxury of having a large pool of people like themselves across the organization, including in influential positions. It is easier to benefit from these similar relationships that may provide both trust and advice/influence. With this understanding, it is no surprise that the "old boys' network" is so effective and hard to compete against.

At an individual level, it is good to be aware of this reality and try to work with it instead of fighting against it. For example, if you are in the minority, you need to be more intentional about building your networks with people in the majority who can provide advice and influence related to organizational activities. You may want to identify specific people to meet, especially outside your immediate group and at more senior levels. Reach out to them, invite them for coffee and try to find common ground through similar interests. Look for opportunities to interact with them outside of work as well, for example through professional organizations, church groups, sports clubs or the school activities of your children. These provide an opportunity to get to know each other in a different context and let them see your range of talents.

Networks relate to promotion and job mobility, and as such, there may be an inherent bias in favor of the majority group. Companies that want more diversity, especially in senior management, may want to help employees expand their networks and build professional sponsor relationships. Encourage your company to create mentoring programs for minority groups or those new in the organization and develop a more explicit sponsorship process. Look for opportunities to set up cross-functional projects or teams to encourage interaction and build relationships between different groups. Finally, think about how to include sessions in learning and development activities to increase awareness of these natural network-building tendencies in order to break the patterns and achieve better outcomes for everyone in the organization.

Mika: Establishing the MedTech Women network

I have been in the medical devices industry for 25 years, first with a manufacturer and now as a venture capitalist. Women make up a significant part of the industry at all levels, but when it comes to pitching, I found that all the VC partners were men. A group of women came together and created a one-day conference[44] and have built a community of women who can exchange ideas and create opportunities. Only 2% of venture capital funding goes to female-led companies. We wanted to support more female entrepreneurs so they are taken seriously by the VCs. I have been fortunate in my career to work with both men and women who have mentored me and helped me grow. One of my big takeaways is that you have to be intentional about building professional relationships and to invest time in staying in touch.

Summary

Effective networks are different for majority and minority groups. Majority groups can build relationships concentrated on people like themselves to provide advice, support, influence, communication and friendship. Minority groups must take a different approach, however, because they are fewer in number, especially in more senior positions. Whereas an open network was related to early promotion for established managers considered legitimate in an organization, this approach was associated with the slowest promotion for groups not considered legitimate in the organization. Minority groups should consider the reality of the old boys' network and understand how they must build networks differently to achieve friendship and social support as well as access to the information and influence provided by networks. Identifying a sponsor to build credibility and navigate the organization is crucial for career advancement.

Questions for consideration

- *Are you in the majority or minority in your organization?* What are the implications for building your network and achieving social support as well as accessing information and influence?

- *If you are among the minority, do you have a sponsor or mentor?* If not, how could you identify someone other than your boss to help you navigate your way through the organization and advance your career?

- *What network building activities and programs could you introduce in your company?* Have you considered programs to build awareness about the different approaches to networks? Could you introduce a mentorship program to help minority groups or those new in your company to integrate more quickly?

5

Job search: Gathering information and seeking referrals

Overview

Weak ties, opening your network to meet new people, and referrals are all important for your job search. Research suggests that job opportunities are found through weak ties or acquaintances who have access to a larger range of opportunities, especially those different from people close to you. Job search experts suggest that 60% of opportunities come from the "hidden market" – jobs that are never advertised and instead come from your network. Referrals are important for building trust through an introduction to a new person or company. Finally, employers may check with mutual contacts to validate your reputation and avoid bad hiring decisions.

Olivier: Networking to change career post-MBA

A few years ago I completed my MBA. Building on 10 years of experience in engineering, finance and IT with both banks and startups, my goal was to change careers from entrepreneur to intrapreneur in a larger company. I knew that the traditional on-campus recruiting program as well as job postings on LinkedIn or Indeed.com were unlikely to help me. I would have to enhance my networking skills to get my dream job.

I am not a natural networker, so first I had to overcome my hesitations. I set a goal of allocating five minutes every day for reaching out to people because effective networking relies on having a routine. I identified potential areas of credibility, for example within my classmates, our alumni network and with former colleagues who knew my talents and could refer me to people who could help. In the end, I found my dream job as a corporate development manager in M&A and strategic planning, a position that perfectly mixed my experiences in technology, startups and corporate and built on the skills acquired in my MBA program.

Now I share my experience with current MBA students. Some of the tips I give them are:

- *Define your job search objectives, recognizing that this is a dynamic process*

- *Identify the matchmakers in your class and get on their radar screen*

- *Hunt in a tribe with your class, i.e. go to networking events as a group and look out for opportunities for everyone*

- *Be a giver and be willing to help future generations*

- *Thank you notes and updates are appreciated*

I also see that networking continues to be important in an organizational context. Within a company, the network provides opportunities to gather feedback and secure your position, to build partnerships, to contact outsiders who face similar business issues and to be known in the industry by headhunters.

The research

Networks and networking are critical in the job search process. Job search experts suggest that 60% of opportunities come through the hidden job market – they are never advertised and come through word of mouth. Networks are the way to access this informal market, which often has more interesting opportunities and the potential to shape a job aligned with your talents and the needs of the organization.[45]

One of the most famous pieces of networks research is called "the strength of weak ties." Far more job seekers found positions through distant acquaintances (28%) than through close contacts, identified as people they saw at least twice a week (17%). This research suggested that strong ties provide bonds, while weak ties provide bridges. People with whom you have strong ties are likely to have the same information sources as you, while weak ties come from a wider variety of sources and have more diverse access to potential jobs. In addition, because weak ties require less effort to maintain, they provide more efficient access to information.[46]

The book *What Color is your Parachute?* suggests that when employers hunt for candidates, they prefer someone trusted. The largest percentage of new jobs comes from promotion within, giving proof of your skills, or from a recommendation by a colleague or friend. The smallest percentage comes from an agency, a job ad or sending a résumé or CV.[47] Access either through your direct network or a referral gives you more job opportunities.

When a company is about to make a hiring decision, your network reputation plays a role. References are fine, but anyone who provides a reference is likely to give a positive one. A better screening mechanism for HR professionals is to look on LinkedIn or Facebook to identify mutual connections (especially former peers or subordinates) and ask those people about the candidate's work and reputation.[48] Information gathered in this way is more likely to give an accurate reflection of character. Because the negative impact of a taker typically exceeds the positive impact of a giver by a multiple of two or three to one, the best way to increase the productivity of an organization is to eliminate takers. For companies, avoiding hiring "takers" by gathering reputational information pays off significantly, so maintaining a good reputation is critical to get a job.

Practical implications

In the job search process, the objective of networking is to collect information, validate your career prospects and expand your range of contacts. This should be done through "warm calls," i.e. people you know or people who refer you. Only when you have gathered sufficient information about your target company or job are you ready to approach the hidden market to ask for an interview. At this stage, if you can find the right person to approach that can make all the difference.[49]

Job seekers understand the importance of networking, yet many feel uncomfortable engaging in it. For example, university students were asked to identify two positive and two negative elements related to networking.[50] They saw clear benefits of networking related to meeting and connecting with people, gathering information, more job leads and career advancement, and overall the potential for creating opportunities (see *Figure 6*).

Figure 6. Positive benefits of networking

Source: EHL Career Workshop[50]

At the same time, they identified challenges related to networking as feeling superficial and fake, unease with meeting strangers and starting conversations, feeling awkward, shy and uncomfortable, and the time-consuming nature of following up and maintaining relationships (see *Figure 7*).

Having a strategy and a plan for approaching job search networking activities is one way to overcome these fears.

Weak ties, opening your network to meet new people, and referrals are important for your job search. If you want to reestablish contact with your weak ties, think about reaching out to them for coffee, asking if they have time for a telephone or Skype call or going back to the organization or activities where you met. Rather than asking straight out for a job, if you ask for advice about whom to contact or ideas for your job search, most people are happy to help. When you go to events, reconnecting with weak ties may be as beneficial as meeting new people

51

because you can reestablish the connection. Many people are relieved to see someone they know and are happy to catch up and provide information for your job search.

Figure 7. Challenges related to networking

Source: EHL Career Workshop[50]

If you want to open your network to meet new contacts, consider having lunch with new people at work, attending events or joining new organizations. You can identify potential new contacts by searching LinkedIn or alumni directories. Look for people in your target function, industry or company. If they are alumni of your university, you can reach out to them directly and ask for their advice. If you do not have an immediate affiliation, look for someone you know who could make an introduction.

Referrals, often coming through weak ties, are also key to a successful job search. Identify people who know you or are similar to you, for example alumni, former colleagues or friends from extracurricular activities. They may be able to introduce you to people in their networks who can provide insights and advice. An introduction opens a path that might otherwise be slow to access because you build on the reputation of the person who referred you to smooth the way.

Finally, trust is an important element in networking for your job search. Building on the trust of a referrer can smooth your introduction to a company. Trust builds over time, and a job offer often comes after many interview rounds over several weeks or months. When it comes time for hiring, you need a good reputation, especially with peers and subordinates, because companies want to avoid bad hiring decisions. People hire those they trust, and if you don't have trust with an employer, either directly or through your network, nothing else matters.

Ruud: Most people underestimate the importance of networking in their job search

When starting their job search, most people underestimate the importance of networking. As a headhunter, I suggest that candidates do not feel shy to ask for leads and that they build multiple identities, for example as a researcher, a solution provider or an expert on a specific topic. This allows a candidate to have conversations around a topic, not around a job search.

Andreas: Building on referrals for internal career growth

About two years after joining a Big 4 accounting firm, I started exploring opportunities for an assignment in Asia. The standard way to do this was to enter an application into a database and then hope for the best. I chose a different route. I had built good credibility with a senior partner in the firm by supporting one of his key accounts. So I contacted this partner, told him that I would be interested in an Asian assignment and asked if he could help me establish the relevant connections. Instead of recommending me directly to partners in Asia, he allowed me to take part in a conference, where these partners would be present.

At the three-day conference, I met a number of Asian partners and presented my case. What followed was an invitation to Singapore to meet the partners there. In the end, I got a good international assignment with much better conditions than people who had applied via the database system.

Paul: Being referred for a job while organizing networking events

During a period of career transition, I decided to organize a business networking group. I organized several monthly events featuring speakers on a range of different topics. During this time, I partnered with a friend to organize a fundraising event following the terrible tsunami in the Indian Ocean. We pulled in volunteers from the networking group to help. A couple of weeks later, following one of these networking events, a member of the group who had helped manage the finances for the fundraising event asked if I would be interested in pursuing an opening in the NGO where he worked. The existing relationship combined with the opportunity to see me in action, led to a job opportunity and a career change that I would never have considered otherwise.

Summary

Networks and networking are critical to access the hidden job market that represents 60% of potential opportunities. This happens most often through weak ties, opening your network to meet new people, and referrals. Networking to search for a job is about gathering information (not asking for a job); good strategies for this are meeting new people through direct outreach combined with referrals. Employers want to avoid bad hiring decisions, so maintaining a good reputation within your network and building trust are important to ensure that you get the job.

Questions for consideration

- *What is your job search goal?* Who do you know who could help you with information or advice so you can learn more? Is there someone who could refer you to these people?

- *Do you have a networking plan?* What activities performed daily, weekly or monthly would help you to reach your objectives?

- *What is your reputation?* Have you developed a good reputation, especially with your peers and subordinates, so that when employers investigate informally, they hear positive things about you?

6

Organizations: Networks for change and innovation

Overview

Organizational networks are different from the organization chart. They are the informal connections between people and how they interact with each other in areas such as advice, trust, support and influence. People play different roles in organizational networks – for example, group central connector, boundary spanner, information broker and peripheral specialist – and each of these roles brings certain resources to the organization. Informal networks contribute to change and innovation and central connectors have the greatest ability to facilitate change. Mixed networks, with weak ties and diverse connections outside the organization combined with strong ties inside the organization, provide the greatest opportunity for innovation.

Peter: Mixing a network to facilitate innovation

After 20 years' experience in a major multinational company, I was tapped for a project to be the central connector between five business units of the organization. Each of these groups had a particular interest in the growth potential for a certain product, but this potential could not be effectively realized due to vested interests and competing priorities. I knew the answer could be found by connecting with 12 countries around the world.

With the support of top management, I introduced myself to the market heads who made time in their agenda to see me at short notice, given the strategic nature of the product. These heads identified key people in their businesses, and I interviewed 5 or 6 people in each country, speaking with 60 different people in total. I could see the value of the network both in opening the door for the initial connections as well as in unblocking bottlenecks. When it felt like stakeholders were stalling on the final outcome, my sponsor leveraged his network to ensure the conclusions and way forward were endorsed by the stakeholders. The outcome of this project was a white paper that still today is considered the reference for this strategic product innovation.

The research

Organizational networks: People play different roles

Networks inside organizations are different from individual networks. Being in the same organization, you know and interact with many people who are connected to each other. Additionally, informal social networks are different than the formal organization chart. Advice networks reveal the experts in an organization, while trust networks identify those who can facilitate change.[51] People play different roles in organizational networks as described below.[52]

- *Group central connectors*: People in the center of the network who are connected to the greatest number of people. In most cases, central connectors are not the formally designated go-to people in the company.

- *Boundary spanners*: People who nurture connections mainly with those outside the informal network, for example communicating with people in other departments within a company, at different satellite offices or in other organizations.

- *Information brokers:* People who connect the various subnetworks, without whom the network as a whole would not exist.

- *Peripheral specialists*: People who operate on the periphery of the network and have specific kinds of information or technical knowledge, for example research data, software skills or customer expertise. They play an important role as experts and may bring new ideas into the organization.

Each of these roles can help or hinder information flow and work getting done. For example, a social network analysis (see *Figure 8*) revealed the network of a group providing thought leadership and specialized support to a company's knowledge management consultants. It included people either with advanced university degrees or extensive industry experience in strategy and organizational design or in technical fields such as data warehousing or information architecture. The group was created to integrate these capabilities and create a holistic knowledge management solution. The partner in charge, however, felt intuitively that the group was not leveraging its talents as effectively as possible.[53]

The group on the left was skilled in the "softer" issues of organizational design and strategy, while the group on the right was more expert in the "harder" technical aspects of knowledge management, such as information architecture, modeling and data warehousing. Each subgroup worked well together, but there was little cross-group information exchange or collaboration, and there was a bottleneck with the boundary spanner in the middle. The group central connectors of the subgroups were keeping the group together, while the peripheral specialists were bringing in new information from outside the organization for the core part of the network to build upon.

Figure 8. Roles in an organizational network

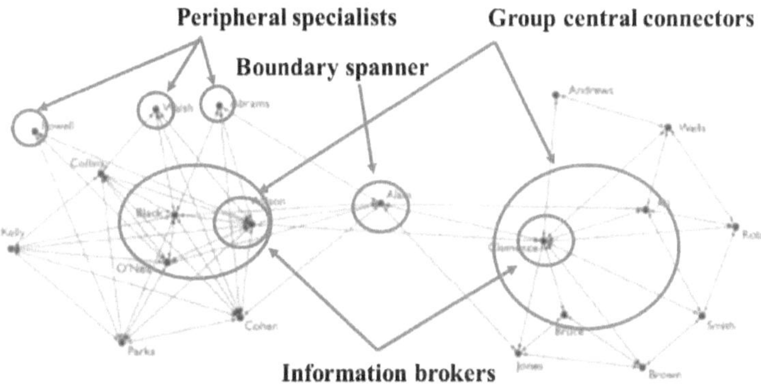

Source: Cross, Borgatti and Parker (2002)[53]

An organization that identifies blockages in its informal network can take action to improve relationships and evolve the network. In the network above, the company took steps over the course of nine months to improve the relationships across groups. Specifically, it:

57

- *Staffed internal projects jointly* with one person from each group (i.e. for writing white papers and developing a project-tracking database). People had to work together and develop an appreciation of each other's unique skill and knowledge.

- *Implemented mixed revenue sales goals* making each manager accountable for selling projects that included both a technical and an organizational component. People had to find ways to integrate their approaches to address client problems.

- *Created new communication forums* including weekly status calls, short weekly email updates and a project tracking database that helped members stay up to date with the group's activities.

- *Changed organization structure* to remove information blockers.

These interventions were significant. Over the course of the next several months, the group began to sell more work that integrated the skills of both groups, and this integration was a differentiator compared with the competition. Nine months later, the new network diagram looked like the one shown in *Figure 9*.[54]

Figure 9. Organizational network post-intervention

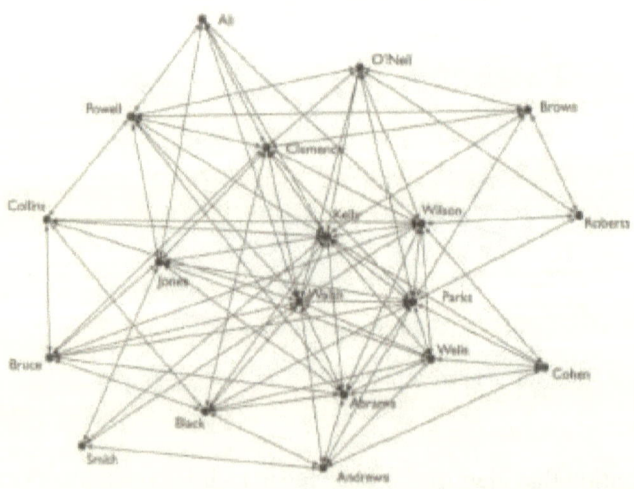

Source: Cross, Borgatti and Parker (2002) [53]

58

Central connectors for change, mixed networks for innovation

Research also suggests that informal networks contribute to change and innovation as illustrated in *Figure 10.*[55]

Figure 10. Networks play a role in change and innovation

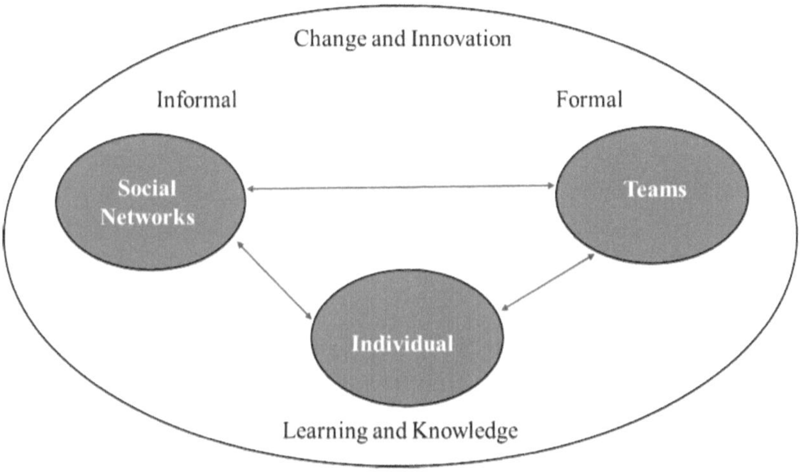

Source: Liedtka (2016)[55]

In research studying change networks in the UK's National Health Service (NHS), an individual's position in the organizational network related strongly with their ability to facilitate change. Being a central connector was a predictor of change agent success at every organizational level. Network structure played a role in change success, and the right structure depended on the type of change needed. Specifically, more open or bridging networks were important for dramatic reforms, while more connected or cohesive networks facilitated changes that built on existing organizational norms. If a person's network was not right for the change initiative, they could consider partnering with someone with a better network fit to increase the chance of achieving the change objectives.[56]

When innovation was the goal, teams obtained the best results when they took a mixed network approach, combining the talents of central connectors with those of peripheral specialists and boundary spanners. These teams combined the benefits of diverse external networks to gather information from the market with cohesive internal networks that allowed them to commercialize these ideas.[57]

In addition, innovation performance related to relationship strength, such that weak ties outside the organization generating a range of different ideas, combined with strong ties inside the organization, provided the trust to share the knowledge and commercialize the ideas.[58] For example, innovative design firms in alliance networks integrated a large number of diverse weak ties with a core of strong ties. Interacting with several design firms at the same time fostered learning, the rapid accumulation of individual skills and the organizational capabilities to manage collaborative relationships. Companies with this approach had greater openness to market trends, built trust through repeated interactions, and developed exclusive agreements with a narrow and well-defined scope.[59]

A similar mixing approach was found beneficial among employees classified as *innovators* or *adaptors* who had different skills that related in different ways with innovative performance. Innovators reframed and recombined problems to generate novel ideas, and although the ideas might be brilliant, they sometimes struggled to gain support for them. Adaptors, in contrast, framed ideas in ways that were acceptable to others to facilitate implementation. Their more consensual approach, however, sometimes impeded recombination and novel idea generation. Innovative performance related either to an innovative style matched with a connected network to support the innovator or to an adaptive style combined with an open network to discover novel connections.[60] This mixed network approach facilitated better innovation outcomes.

One way to implement this mixed network approach would be to combine peripheral specialists with central connectors. The peripheral specialists have contacts outside the organization – salespeople interacting with clients, an innovation team searching for new ideas, or strategic collaborations with universities for research and technology. The goal of these teams is to gather lots of diverse information that might be transformed into innovative new products. In order to design something that works and can be sold, however, these ideas need to be passed through to smaller, connected teams with stronger ties. These teams have the mutual trust to debate the ideas, share the tacit knowledge to refine them and to transform the ideas into a feasible product. Combining the strengths of market access by peripheral specialists and innovators with the trust and organizational skills of central connectors and adaptors in development teams can transform the ideas into real innovations.

Practical implications

Given the influence of informal social networks on organizational performance, you may want to map your group's organizational network following the guidelines in Chapter 9. This will help you to understand the roles played by different team members and potential bottlenecks or areas of resistance that could be improved through specific interventions.

Consider how you could enhance the connections between group members, for example, by the design of your physical office space, by creating activities for people to get to know each other, or by how you staff cross-functional projects. Changes such as an open office design, strategically placed coffee machines, or mixing teams most likely to benefit from interaction on the same floor could enhance communication between team members. Consider creating budgets for travel, social activities or team building exercises to encourage your employees to get to know each other and build stronger relationships. You might also consider creating a company directory that makes it easy to identify experts and encourage people to contact each other for advice. At McKinsey, for example, knowledge sharing is encouraged by a policy requiring a response within 24 hours to any colleague sending a request for help.[61]

If your corporate objective is change, identify the central connectors in your organizational network, especially those with the right skills for your change initiative to increase your chance of success. If your objective is innovation, a mixed network can be particularly beneficial. Consider how to leverage diverse external contacts outside the company to gather information combined with strong ties and connected networks inside the company to allow these ideas to germinate. Think of an image of fennel – a vegetable rich in vitamins and minerals. The green stalks represent the external relationships of team members, stretching out into

61

the world for light and air, i.e. new ideas. They bring these ideas back to the core white bulb, the close team, who can combine these ideas and grow something solid and fruitful.

Jordi: Networks help you grow, and they need to be nurtured

In a career of 29 years with a large automobile manufacturer (found through my network) I had different assignments, many related to my ambition and performance. They all happened, and perhaps the most important ones, thanks to the relationships I had "webbed" (at that time the word network was not used) within the company. Thanks to this I moved for an expatriation to Paris that was supposed to last for three years... I have been on that journey ever since.

In my last years in the company I was convinced that by doing a good job and due to my experience, I had momentum enough to make it to the end, kind of forgetting the relationship aspect. This resulted in a dry network, combined with an advanced age that led to a mutual agreement of departure. It helped me realize that good work is never enough if not supported by a good network. Strong learning.

Summary

Knowing how organizational networks function can help you understand how to get things done or, alternatively, why there might be bottlenecks or communication issues. You can take steps to change organizational networks through proactive actions such as the office layout, team building exercises and assigning people to specific projects to expand their network and share ideas. If you are central in your network, you have a better chance of implementing change. Innovation is facilitated by mixed networks combining the strengths of those inside and outside the organization as well as the talents of innovators and adaptors for greater innovation performance.

Questions for consideration

- ***Do you know how your team or organization is connected to each other?*** Who are the experts that people go to for advice? Who do they trust? What role do you play?

- ***Would you like to be more central in your network?*** If so, what specific actions could you take to meet new people, deepen your relationships and create more energy?

- ***Would your organization benefit from a more connected network?*** What actions could you take to encourage more interaction between groups including the physical office layout, team building activities or cross-functional teams?

- ***What is the network structure and innovation style of your innovation team?*** Do you have open networks outside the organization to gather new ideas linked to connected networks inside the organization to commercialize these ideas? Do you have both innovators and adaptors who can work together to generate new ideas and get them accepted by potential customers and investors?

Part 3: Networking Tools and Techniques

Although not the core of your networking activities, events and technology do play a role in your networking plan, especially for meeting new people and staying connected.

Key concepts you will learn are:

- *Networking events* are more productive and more enjoyable when you have a plan and when you approach them in a calm and authentic way. Staying in "second circle" and engaging with open groups are some ideas.

- *Networking technologies* such as LinkedIn, Facebook and Twitter are helpful for identifying new people to meet, learning about their backgrounds to find common interests and staying in touch. They are also useful for content creation and dissemination to build your reputation.

- *Face-to-face interactions and follow-up* over coffee or through shared activities remain critical for more in-depth relationship building.

7

Networking events: Before, during and after

Overview

Networking is frequently associated with meeting new people by attending as many events as possible. As discussed previously, in reality networking is about building relationships, and the superficial nature of events is not conducive to this. Events *do* play a role in a networking plan, however, especially to meet new people or to reconnect with weak ties. Attending an industry event, for example, where participants share common interests may facilitate connections that could be developed following the event. Technology such as LinkedIn helps you to prepare for and stay connected after an event.

Nathalie: Networking groups with practical connecting activities

I belong to a networking group where meetings are designed to encourage people to get to know each other. At each bi-monthly meeting, the group gets together to discuss a business topic, so participants have a genuine reason for attending the event. Direct business promotion is prohibited, however. At the end of the meeting, each person draws a Scrabble letter with two of each in the bag. Members find their letter match, and before the next meeting, they must organize an informal follow up meeting to know each other better. At this point business information can be exchanged. In this way, members are building relationships over coffee instead of handing out business cards – a much more effective approach.

The research

Events are the activity most associated with networking, even though they play a relatively small part in your portfolio of activities. For some people, attending large group functions puts them outside their comfort zone, and they describe the experience with words such as awkward, fake, pressure, small-talk and uncomfortable. The good news is that with some preparation and practice, networking events can become less daunting and can even begin to be fun.

Preparation before the event helps to identify interesting people and learn something about them. For example, you can identify two or three things to learn at the function and then study the participant list in advance and check the backgrounds of interesting people using social media. With this preparation in your back pocket, on the day of the event, you can relax and be yourself, smile and be friendly and focus on giving. According to Michael Port, an expert in communication and business development, you should think about these tips for your conversations: [62]

- Introduce yourself to the person hosting the event or someone you want to meet
- Offer something when first meeting them, for example, praise, compassion or connection
- Start conversations by asking questions
- Be inclusive by asking others to join your conversations
- Ask for a business card of those you've met and follow up with them afterwards with an email or requesting a LinkedIn connection.

There are also some things not to do at networking events. For example, don't:

- Try to be cool and brag about your success
- Ask "What do you do?" as your first question
- Sit with people you know for the majority of the event
- Have multiple items in your hands
- Complain – about anything
- Take yourself too seriously – relax and have fun.

Being present in "second circle"[63] is a concept from the acting world that applies well to networking activities. In "first circle" people are withdrawn and self-focused, making them uninteresting. In contrast, someone in "third circle" is all about bluff and force, making them so overbearing as to be uninteresting as well. Someone in "second circle" exhibits an energy of connecting. They are centered and calm, interested in listening to others and much more likely to have a positive experience and come away with new potential relationships.

Having a strategy on whom to approach can also help to make the event more enjoyable. Networking expert Christopher Barrat suggests that open groups of three people who are facing out toward the room are the easiest to join (as compared to facing each other). If you need further help getting into an established group, look for people standing near a table where you can set down your drink. At least the person near the table should open up so you can start a conversation. Avoid closed groups with three or four people huddled together, as these will be the least receptive to interruptions.[64]

After a networking event, be sure to follow up with the people you met. Ideally you have exchanged business cards so that you have their email address or other contact details. It is also a good opportunity to connect on LinkedIn to make it easy to stay in touch. If you promised to send them something, such as an article or idea, be sure to include that in your follow-up note.

Practical implications

If you are organizing a networking event, you may want to include specific activities to help attendees maximize their chances of meeting people. For example, circulating the participant list in advance lets participants identify interesting people to meet and check their backgrounds. Speed networking or proactively connecting people with similar interests may be a way to break the ice, especially in a group where participants don't know each other. For speed networking, ask people to move and introduce themselves to someone new each time the bell rings, say every 3 minutes. A few rounds are enough to get the energy flowing and help people feel comfortable with introductions. You might consider a Reciprocity Ring, where individuals identify a personal or professional challenge and the group suggests people or ideas to help.

Another idea is to give participants a challenge for the event to speak to at least three people they did not know before. This simple rule provides relief for those less comfortable with meeting new people because everyone must do it. Or you could consider drawing Scrabble letters from a bag to provide a structured process for post-meeting follow-up. Finally, think about how to sequence event activities to provide an opportunity for mixing as well as time for smaller group discussions. In this way participants have a chance to get to know a range of people as well as the possibility to talk more deeply to specific people with mutual interests.

Keep in mind that meeting or reconnecting with someone at an event is only the first step. The real value comes afterward, when you follow up to organize a discussion over coffee, via Skype or another activity. It is through these face-to-face, relationship-building activities that your networking efforts have the greatest potential for impact.

Benedikt: Reconnecting with people I know at networking events

Just today I met someone at an event. I have known the person for a long time, so it was not so much the actual networking event, but rather the occasion to meet someone I knew to raise the subject that perhaps a specific opportunity could be of interest to him. He knew about it, but the fact of meeting me in person made him think seriously about it, and there is a good chance of him signing up.

Peggy: Setting a plan to meet people in the industry and in a new city

My first real networking event was an international conference, where my manager was the speaker and wanted a female employee in the audience. I decided to get out of my comfort zone and, during every break, made it a goal to speak to new people and sit at a table where I did not know a single person.

On a personal level, I do my best to surround myself with positive people that can lift me up, just as I enjoy lifting other people up. When I moved to a new city, I joined Events and Adventures (E&A) – a club for singles with events every day of the week, all different activities like rock climbing, sport, parties, karaoke, etc. Here I learned the value of finding friends in a new city that have the same interests and values I have. I am no longer in

E&A, as you must leave when you get married, but just yesterday, I met up with some of my best friends – most of them from E&A.

Nathalie: An approach of connecting with people and helping others

In the past when attending networking events, I would have a specific objective in mind, for example "How can they help me to land the job?" or to buy services. This approach was very much about gathering business cards and having rather superficial conversations. Now, my main goal is to connect with people. For me, connecting means getting to know the person on a deeper level and ideally "serving" them. Having said that, serving does not mean making them my client; it means really understanding who they are and what their needs are. I am always holding the question "How can I help this person?" in the back of my mind. Sometimes, I help through my business but mostly *it means introducing them to someone in my network who can possibly help them. It's not about me, it's about them!*

This approach, in my opinion, has two benefits. First, I feel good about helping someone, as this is a key value of mine. Second, more often than not, by helping them, they remember me and when they meet someone who may need my services, they make the introduction. This approach obviously takes longer than the "please buy from me" approach, but I believe it pays off with more value in the long run. Networking in this way has taken all the pressure off "getting the sale" and made it way more fun!

Nora: Spontaneous participation leads to professional partnership

I spontaneously decided to participate in a Book Yourself Solid event simply because the content in Michael Port's book of the same name resonated strongly with me. Although I didn't know the organizer or any other participants, most of the people I met at the event shared similar values and interests so we easily found a good tone. After the event, I simply enjoyed keeping in touch with these people for mutual inspiration and friendship. Completely unexpectedly, this also led to a valuable job referral and a professional partnership.

My approach to building my network always has been to focus on building friendships and meaningful connections because I was not very good at promoting myself or cultivating contacts purely for business reasons. Earlier in my career, I thought I was doing something wrong since I wasn't able to connect with the people I thought I needed to connect with in order to develop my business. It is a big relief and a lot less stressful to know that I'm actually doing the right thing when I simply focus on building friendships and genuine connections without any ulterior motives.

Summary

Networking events are helpful when you need to meet new people and gather information, for example in your job search or when you are looking for new ideas. Just getting out may give you energy and momentum. Having a strategy about how to navigate networking events may make them more comfortable, and approaching them in "second circle" will help you feel more centered and confident. If you are organizing an event, building in time for meeting new people as well as for more in-depth discussions will make follow-up among participants more likely and your event more valuable. After events, think about how you can follow up with interesting people over coffee to get to know them better and start to build a stronger relationship.

Questions for consideration

- *Are there networking events that you could benefit from attending?* Which events or groups would help you to gather information related to your goal?

- *What are two or three things you would like to learn at the event?* How can you identify people you would like to meet so you can find out more about them beforehand?

- *Are you designing events for effective networking?* How can you structure your events both to encourage mixing and to create opportunities for small group or in-depth discussions?

- *What actions can you take after events to follow up with interesting people?* Send them a LinkedIn request or thank you note? Send them an interesting article related to your discussion? Invite them for coffee?

71

8

Networking technology:
LinkedIn, Facebook, Twitter

Overview

The explosion of networking technology in recent years might lead us to wonder whether relationships will soon be developed only virtually. Yet at least in current practice, building relationships face to face remains more significant, even among savvy technology users. Networking technologies such as LinkedIn, Facebook and Twitter are beneficial for maintaining connections with people you already know and for gathering information about potential connections and trends. Research suggests that people have different networking styles via technology, in addition to those identified in Chapter 1, and that social media can be effective for enhancing collaboration, building visibility and improving awareness of current activities. Knowing how to leverage networking technology can enhance your ability to stay in contact with people and increase your awareness-building efforts.

Peter: Using Facebook to target the right clients

For my business development I am using Facebook because I can target people very tightly. There are people in my network who have certain characteristics that match those of my customers. The data on Facebook is pretty granular and describes personal characteristics and interests, as compared to LinkedIn which focuses on professional characteristics and careers. I target specific types of people and share general interest stories about my area of activity, with the idea that they will be curious enough to click on the stories and want to find out more by starting to follow me and my business.

The research

There is a wealth of articles about the practical uses of social media. For example, you can search LinkedIn for tips on how to get the most out of its technology to promote your business, identify potential clients or help with your job search. Limited research, however, has been published linking the terms "social media" and "network," and the research that is published tends to focus more on social media as a marketing tactic and less as a network or relationship building tool. The few articles that do exist describe how people use social media for networking, how social media can be used for awareness building and how people have different networking styles.

One study found that 98% of respondents' online friends were people known from face-to-face interactions. Facebook was perceived to be beneficial for maintaining contact with these people in a more efficient way, especially those who were more distant and with whom regular contact was not maintained, i.e. weak ties. Facebook also was good for facilitating face-to-face activities such as events, with participants recognizing the importance of these activities in relationship building. Online social networking was an extension of relationship building activities in person or by phone, text and email, not a replacement for these activities.[65]

Social media also had value for promoting content and allowed users to: [66]

- Build professional visibility and credibility
- Talk to people or call them more easily as a follower on social media
- Identify interesting events and follow events if it was not possible to participate
- Find information about projects, new trends and ideas
- Follow professionally relevant news anywhere and anytime
- Gain an idea of someone's personality by following their social media activities.

Overall, social media helped to improve collaboration among fellow researchers, to increase the visibility of their work and to enhance their awareness of new developments.

A final study analyzed the motivations of people around affiliation, achievement and power, in relation to their connections on LinkedIn or Xing. It suggested that affiliation-motivated people had a greater number of contacts with people they already knew in person. Those with an achievement motivation tended to have smaller networks focused around colleagues and a greater number of connections with people lower in the hierarchy. Finally, those with a motivation toward power tended to have a larger number of contacts and added strangers to their networks to have an information edge.[67] Thinking back to the networking styles discussed earlier, it seems people have a variety of online networking styles as well.

Practical implications

Social networking technology is helpful for staying connected to people you already know, gathering information and building awareness for you and your business. Social media sites provide good databases to identify people whom you may want to meet or learn more about. If you are looking for new contacts in your industry or region, you may want to do a search for the relevant characteristics to see whom you know or, even better, identify 2nd level connections who could introduce or refer you. LinkedIn and Facebook are also excellent sources of information when preparing for a meeting or interview to understand the background of your contact and identify areas of similar interests or experiences around which you might start a conversation.

Social media sites are useful tools for staying in touch with people, especially those with whom you don't communicate regularly because you have a weak tie relationship. Because people update their own profiles, this virtual address book is adjusted immediately if someone leaves for a new job or moves to another city. They are also effective tools for reconnecting with people from a previous life stage, for example former colleagues or classmates. Technology makes it possible to stay connected without investing large amounts of time, especially with your weaker ties.

Finally, the content features of social network sites make them a good medium for promoting your personal or business activities without being intrusive. Articles or other content posted on social media can be consumed at the discretion of the viewer. They also are spread to your contacts' contacts, which can number several hundred or thousand depending on the size of your network. Even if they do not click on your article, you have landed in their newsfeed and informed them of your expertise.

Kevin: Growing a network as part of content creation

For my business, I use my content creation to open doors. It enables me to interview industry leaders. I learn a great deal from these interviews and this has enabled me indirectly to build my brand among those in this space. I post these stories on my website and promote them through LinkedIn and Twitter, which generates awareness through my network. For the future, I want to continue building on the power of weak ties and growing my network through content creation – and then let the power of serendipity work its magic!

Summary

Social media provides a tool to support your relationship-building activities. It helps to keep you connected with people you already know, especially your weak ties, and it provides a database for identifying potential new connections. Finally, it provides a channel for content dissemination to enhance your visibility with those in your extended network and build their awareness of your expertise. Social media can provide an important support tool for keeping in touch with people in your network, even though your first contact with them is likely to have been face to face.

Questions for consideration

- *Do you have a profile on LinkedIn, Facebook, Twitter or other social media?* What is your strategy for connecting with people? Does an approach of affiliation, achievement or power resonate with you?

- *Do you regularly follow social media posts to stay aware of trends?* How could you devise a focused approach to gathering information without an excessive time investment?

- *Could social media increase your visibility or that of your business?* How could you increase your content contribution to be more visible in your network?

Part 4: Network Analysis and Action Plan

To gain value from your network, you need to understand what it looks like today, how it relates to your objectives and what actions you can take to enhance it for better results. This part provides a step-by-step approach to guide you through the process. Doing it in one sitting takes approximately an hour, but I recommend that you do it in stages, giving yourself time to reflect both on what your network looks like today and, more importantly, what you would like it to look like in the future and specific actions to get there.

Key steps you will follow are:

- **_Define your objectives and situation_**, including types of information you need to gather, characteristics of your industry and country environment, and your reputation and legitimacy.

- **_Chart and analyze your network_** both inside and outside your organization. See how these structures relate to your objective.

- **_Design your future network_** by identifying how you would like to adapt existing relationships. Identify people you would like to add to your network and specific activities you could undertake to build the relationship.

- **_Set specific actions or key performance indicators (KPIs)._** Start with small and consistent steps to help you achieve your goals.

If you want to chart your network using software, UCINet is a comprehensive package. You can download a trial version at http://www.analytictech.com.[68]

If you would like to discuss your results or have specific questions, send me an email janet@top10learningsolutions.com.

9

Charting your network and preparing your plan

Overview

As described in the previous chapters, it is possible to analyze your network to understand how it aligns with your objectives. If there are opportunities to make it better, you can develop a plan to do so. This section includes exercises to define and enhance your network:

1. Define your objectives and situation

2. Analyze and chart your network

3. Design your future network

4. Set specific actions to build relationships

5. Define key performance indicators (KPIs) to achieve your goals

These steps are applied separately to your networks inside and outside your organization. If you are an entrepreneur, searching for a job, looking for new ideas, or working mostly outside your organization, follow the steps to chart your external network. If you want to understand your internal organizational network, follow the steps to see how you are connected to colleagues and the role that you play, i.e. central connector, boundary spanner or peripheral specialist and think about how you might identify a sponsor to help you advance in your career. Following these steps should help you understand your network more strategically so you can develop a plan aligned with your objectives and situation to achieve better outcomes.

Peggy: Connecting with people and building trust

I am very task-oriented, so small talk tended to annoy me when I first started in the maritime industry. But I turned it around to be excited to speak to new people. A good opening line to get people to share, is to ask them genuinely: "How was your weekend or vacation?" "What did you do?" It is refreshing for them to speak to someone who actually cares about them as a person, rather than talking about the weather all day.

Without knowing it, I was networking. I used my empathy, curiosity and interest in people to make my day a little more interesting, despite working in an industry where most things come down to money. I built trust with colleagues, vendors, customers, etc. and when I needed a favor, I got things done. I eventually understood the value, and in my training of other operators, I encouraged them to pick up the phone and connect with people, so they have a network of people ready to help when a challenge comes up.

Networks outside your company: Entrepreneurs, job seekers, idea seekers, working outside your organization

Entrepreneurs, job seekers, those looking for new ideas, and those who work primarily with people outside their organization, for example those in business development, will benefit from this section.

Step 1: Define your objectives and situation and identify the network structure that aligns best

Since the most effective approach to networking depends on your objectives and situation, the first step is to define them.

Start by listing your top 3 objectives for the coming year. These could include meeting people for new ideas, winning new customers, gaining funding or looking for a new job.

NETWORKING: COFFEE NOT COCKTAILS

Top 3 objectives
1.
2.
3.

Then answer these questions related to the different contextual elements. Refer back to Chapter 2 to understand the network structure and relationship approach that fits best with your situation.

Context elements	Network approach
The type of knowledge I need to share is: • Explicit: Data and facts • Tacit: Complex and confidential	Weak ties Strong ties
My industry is: • Constantly changing, exploration • More mature, exploitation	Open network Connected network
My business environment is: • More certain, efficient legal system • Less certain, less efficient legal system	Open network Connected network
My reputation and perceived legitimacy: • I have an established reputation in my industry or country • I am new to my industry or country	Open network Sponsor network

Step 2: Analyze your external network

Considering this in a professional context, think of contacts outside your company. If you are using this for your job search or other context, adapt the questions accordingly. We will look at both the composition and structure of your network, i.e. the people, the roles they play and the benefits they bring.

The people in your network

Think about the people you interact with on a regular basis outside your company on business issues, for example:

- People you ask regularly for **information and advice**
- People who help you to **build or adjust your strategy**
- People who you have **relied on as sources of general industry information**
- People whose **buy-in and support are important** for the success of your initiatives
- People whom you have **worked with previously**, i.e. former colleagues or classmates

List up to 10 people with whom you interact in a way that relates to your objective. Just write the first names, initials or a code name of the people you decide to list.

First name / initials	Contact type (client, supplier, consultant, industry association, friend, etc.)[69]	How close do I feel to this person? (especially close, close, distant)	The level of energy I feel interacting with this person (1-5, low-high)[70]
1.			
2.			
3.			
4.			
5.			
6.			
7.			
8.			
9.			
10.			

How people are connected

Next see how your contacts are connected. List each person's name on the left side. Ask yourself for each pair in your network, "Do these 2 people know each other?" Mark an X in the box if the answer is yes.

AA	AA								
BB		BB							
CC			CC						
DD				DD					
EE					EE				
FF						FF			
GG							GG		
HH								HH	
II									II
JJ										JJ

Now draw the picture of your network.

- Start with you in the middle

- List your connections and draw a line to them

- Connect those in your network who are connected to each other, based on the X's in the chart above

83

YOU

Example

External network connections

AA	AA									
BB		BB								
CC	X		CC							
DD				DD						
EE		X			EE					
FF						FF				
GG			X				GG			
HH						X		HH		
II					X				II	
JJ								X		JJ

External network diagram

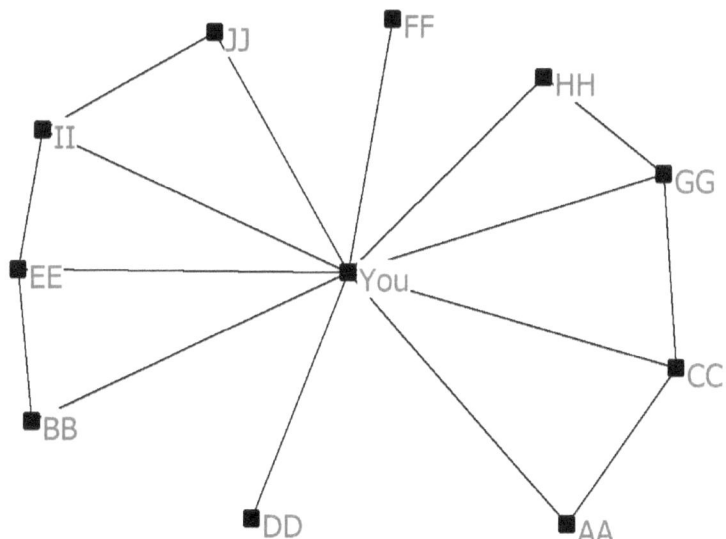

85

Step 3: Design your future network in line with your objectives

Now that you see your network, should it be adjusted in some way to align better with your objectives? For example, should you connect with more people of a specific type? Open your network? Build stronger relationships? Find people to refer you? All of these could be specific actions for you to take going forward.

Three changes to your network

In line with your objectives, write down three things you would like to change to make your network more effective. For example:

- Add contacts of a certain type

- Identify people who can refer me to my target group

- Build stronger relationships with a specific part of my network

3 changes to my network
1.
2.
3.

New people in your network

Now, think about additional people or types of people whom you would like to add to your network. Who are they? For example, would you like to know more people in your industry, meet potential clients and investors, identify people to help with your job search or identify people outside your industry to help with new ideas? Where might you find them? Do you have friends or former colleagues who might have connections? Are there fellow alumni working in your target areas? Who in your 2nd level LinkedIn network could be a source of more opportunities?

List up to 10 new people or types of contacts you would like to add to your network over the next year.

Name or type of contact
1.
2.
3.
4.
5.
6.
7.
8.
9.
10.

Step 4: Build relationships in ways that you enjoy

Now think about how to build relationships with the people in your network, keeping in mind your networking style. Consider what you like best about meeting new people and what you like least. For example

- Do you enjoy meeting people and getting to know them over coffee, at parties or through shared activities?

- Do you prefer interactions in person or via email, telephone or Skype calls?

- How do you like to be referred or to refer others?

You will enjoy building your network – and do it more effectively – if you participate in the activities and communicate in the ways that feel most comfortable for you.

Your relationship-building action plan

When you are ready to make your action plan, consider these ideas related to your specific objectives:

- *Adding contacts of a certain type*: In Step 3 you will have identified the types of contacts you need to meet in order to achieve your goal. Now, search LinkedIn or your alumni directory to identify people who fit your needs. Ask your friends or colleagues if they know anyone. Make a list of the people you would like to meet and decide if you have the credibility to reach out to them directly or if you need to find someone who can refer you. Identify activities or events where you would have a high likelihood of meeting these people and find a way to get involved.

- *Getting referrals*: Once you have identified the people you would like to meet, see if there is anyone in your existing network who could make an introduction. As you ask people in your existing network for ideas, ask them at the same time if they would be willing to introduce you to the contacts they suggest.

- *Building stronger relationships*: Time and intensity are required for stronger relationships. If you want to build stronger connections with those in your current network, consider doing things together outside of your professional relationship. For example, invite someone you know from a professional organization for a coffee or to a sporting event. Or in reverse, invite a friend to join the next speaker event organized by a professional group to which you belong. Consider joining the board of this group so you have to work more closely with people and get to know them better.

- *Be more energizing*: How can you be more constructive and trust-building in your relationships? For example, by listening, responding reliably to emails, being constructive in meetings and building reciprocity in your relationships?

Write down the people you listed previously (existing and new contacts) and think about how to build your relationship with them in the way that works best for both of you.

Name	Specific actions to take
1.	
2.	
3.	
4.	
5.	
6.	
7.	
8.	
9.	
10.	
11.	
12.	
13.	
14.	
15.	

Step 5: Define your networking KPIs

Finally, as with any objective, it good to set yourself some KPIs or tasks to be sure you achieve them. Write down 3 networking goals to get you started and be as specific as possible. Examples could be:

- Contact at least X people every day/week

- Invite X people each week to meet in person over coffee

- Attend 1 new activity every month/quarter

- Spend more quality time with specific people

- Be more energizing in my daily activities by doing Y

3 networking goals/KPIs
1.
2.
3.

By following the guidelines described above, you will develop a networking strategy aligned with your objectives and an action plan to achieve them. If you implement your KPIs through a consistent process, you are more likely to achieve your goal.

Networks inside your organization: Your role, being central, establishing legitimacy

This section discusses networks inside your company and may be most interesting for those who want to learn more about their role, who want to become more central in the organizational network and those in the minority group (women, those of a different racial group, expats or those new in the organization) who need to establish their legitimacy.

Step 1: Define your objectives and situation and identify the network structure that aligns best

As discussed previously, the most effective approach to networking depends on your objectives and situation, so the first step is to define them.

Start by listing your top 3 objectives for the coming year. These could include meeting people, becoming more central in the network, obtaining a promotion, building stronger relations with colleagues, or connecting different parts of your organization.

Top 3 objectives
1.
2.
3.

Then answer these questions related to the different contextual elements. Refer back to chapters 4 and 7 to understand the network structure and relationship approach that fits best with your situation.

Context elements	Network approach
The type of knowledge I need to share is: • Explicit: Data and facts • Tacit: Complex and confidential	 Weak ties Strong ties
My reputation and perceived legitimacy: • I am part of the majority group and/or have an established reputation in my company • I am part of a minority group and/or new to my company	 Open network Sponsor network
The role I play in my organizational network is:	Central connector Boundary spanner Information broker Peripheral specialist

Step 2: Chart your internal organization network

How you are connected to people inside your organization relates to your ability to facilitate change. Start by drawing this network as described below. What is your role? Central connector? Boundary spanner? Peripheral specialist? If that is not your preferred role, what would you need to change? Remember that people more central in the network are more likely to facilitate change in the organization.

Once you have identified the people in your network, consider the benefits they provide. These benefits relate back to chapter 4 and could include advice, friendship, trust or influence. How close do you feel to these people? Are the interactions energizing?

Estimate how people in your organization set are connected to each other following these steps:

People in your network

- Write down everyone in your organization set.

- Write down what type of support they provide, how close you feel to them and the level of energy you feel interacting with each person

Just write the first names, initials or a code name of the people whom you decide to list.

First name / initials	What type of support do they provide you with? (advice, trust, influence, friendship, etc.)	How close do I feel to this person? (especially close, close, distant)	The level of energy I feel interacting with this person (1-5, low-high)
1.			
2.			
3.			
4.			
5.			
6.			
7.			
8.			
9.			
10.			

How people are connected

Now identify how people are connected:

- For each person, estimate the responses to the question "Who do you go to for advice when you have a work- related problem or a decision to make? Mark an X in each appropriate box. (You can also estimate a trust, friendship or influence network, for example by instead asking the question "Who do you trust?") For purposes of this exercise count the connection, even if it is one-directional.

- Count the number of X's for each person by going across the row and down the column associated with them. Those with a greater number have greater centrality.

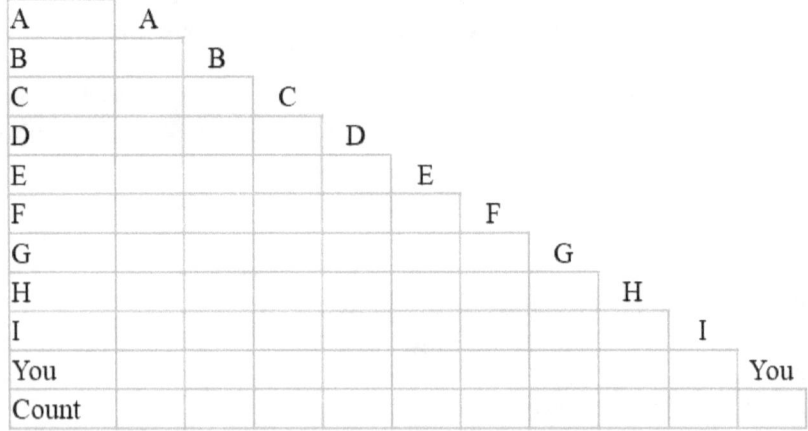

Now draw the picture of your internal network:

- Start with those who have the most X's and put them in the center

- Add a circle for each connection, with those having fewer X's being farther from the center

- Draw a line connecting those whom you have identified as going to each other for advice (even if it goes just in one direction)

- Where do you fit? What is your role?

94

CENTRAL CONNECTORS

Example

Internal network connections

	A	B	C	D	E	F	G	H	I	You
A	A									
B	X	B								
C			C							
D	X	X	X	D						
E					E					
F	X					F				
G	X			X			G			
H					X	X		H		
I									I	
You	X	X	X	X				X	X	You
Count	5	3	2	5	1	2	2	3	1	6

Internal network diagram

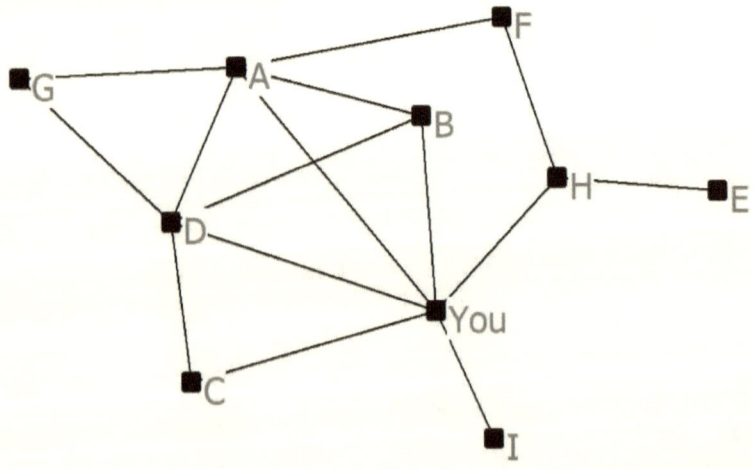

Step 3: Design your future network in line with your objectives

Now that you see your network within your organization, do you want to adjust it in some way to align better with your objectives? For example, should you open your network? Connect with more people? Build stronger relationships? Find a sponsor? Be more central? All of these could be specific actions for you to take going forward.

Three changes to your network

In line with your objectives, write down three things you would like to change to make your network more effective. For example:

- Open my network to meet more people in different parts of my company

- Build stronger relationships with a specific part of my network

- Identify a sponsor who can introduce me to a new group or help me build my credibility

- Be more central in my network

- Connect parts of my network to get to know each other better

3 changes to my network
1.
2.
3.

New people in your network

Now, think about additional people or types of people whom you would like to add to your network. List up to 10 new contacts or types of contacts you would like to add to your internal organizational network or get to know better over the next year. For example, you may want to

97

connect with someone in a different part of your organization whom you know by name and want to meet in person. Or you may have met someone a few times and would like to establish a stronger relationship.

Name	Where in your organization
1.	
2.	
3.	
4.	
5.	
6.	
7.	
8.	
9.	
10.	

Step 4: Build relationships in ways that you enjoy

Now think about how to build relationships with the people in your network, keeping in mind your networking style. Consider what you like best about meeting new people and what you like least. For example

- Do you enjoy meeting people and getting to know them over coffee or over lunch?

- Do you enjoy working on teams or participating in activities together, or do you prefer more informal activities such as drinks after work?

- Do you prefer interactions in person or via email, telephone or Skype calls?

- How do you like to be referred or to refer others?

You will enjoy building your network – and do it more effectively –if you participate in the activities that feel most comfortable for you.

Your relationship building action plan

When you are ready to make your action plan, consider these ideas related to specific objectives:

- *Opening your network*: Formal development activities could include attending an executive development course to meet new people, participating in cross-functional teams or attending industry conferences. Informal development activities could be setting goals to meet a certain number of new people each week or month or attending company social activities.

- *Building relationships with a sponsor/mentor*: Developmental relationships help employees to learn from experience and to build credibility within an organization. Formal development could include identifying a mentor within the organization and defining activities and a plan to get to know each other and provide support. Mentoring can have benefits both ways. For example, senior managers can provide guidance to younger colleagues on how to navigate the organization. In return, junior managers can provide guidance upward about the motivations of millennials or the impact of new technology. Informal activities could be identifying people who might be willing to share their wisdom with you and inviting them for a coffee or offering something to help them in return.

- *Being more central in your network*: Look at your network graph and identify the people who are central and whom you would like to know better. Ask them to lunch or for coffee and/or ask for their advice on business issues. Build your reputation as someone people turn to for advice or trust, especially with energizing behaviors.

- ***Building stronger relationships***: Time and intensity are required for stronger relationships. Identify people in your organization whom you would like to know better and reach out. Formal development could include understanding your relationship style and how to interact with others to build stronger relationships. It could include goals to spend more time with colleagues through team building activities or on specific project teams. Attend more informal social activities or do things together outside of work to build stronger relationships by adding a new layer to your professional relationship.

- ***Be more energizing***: Enhance your relationships by listening, responding promptly to emails, being constructive in meetings and building reciprocity.

Write down the people you listed previously (existing and new contacts) and think about how to build your relationship with them in the best way possible.

Name	Specific actions to take
1.	
2.	
3.	
4.	
5.	
6.	
7.	
8.	
9.	
10.	
11.	
12.	
13.	
14.	
15.	

Step 5: Define your networking KPIs

With internal networks, as with external, it good to set yourself some KPIs or tasks to be sure you achieve your objectives. Write down 3 networking goals to get you started and be as specific as possible. Examples could be:

- Invite X people each week to meet in person over coffee

- Organize X activities for my team to get to know each other better

- Spend quality time with specific people

- Be more energizing in my daily activities by doing Y

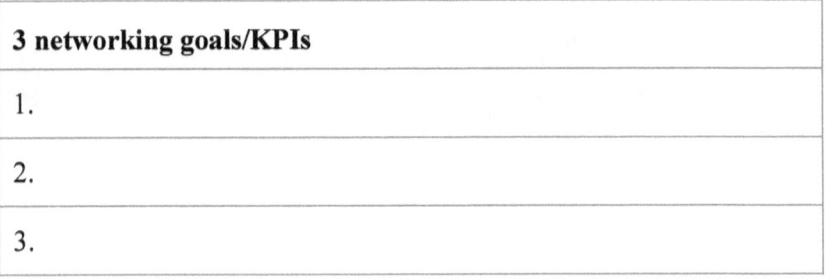

3 networking goals/KPIs
1.
2.
3.

By following the guidelines described above, you will develop a networking strategy aligned with your objectives and an action plan to achieve them. This will help you to navigate your organization more effectively. If you implement your KPIs through a consistent process, you are more likely to achieve your goal.

Mika: Take things step by step

When you want to develop your network, take small steps. You don't have to implement your plan all at once. It is helpful to have clear intentions about what you are trying to do and set some priorities. Start small and then see how things grow.

102

Grady: Meeting people in the restaurant car

Over my 40-year career, all of my jobs and clients (except one) have come through my network. This includes four education-related jobs followed by a transition to entrepreneurship where 100 out of 101 clients have come through connections or referrals. I have done no formal marketing. I find it interesting to meeting new people and try to listen as much as possible in business development lunches. My goal is to engage with people in a genuine way. To be fully engaged for an hour, making them feel that they are the most important thing in the world.

One way I have grown in my approach to networking is that now I speak with strangers on the train, something outside my comfort zone. I have a 1.5-hour train journey approximately three times per week, and I sit in the restaurant car. Over coffee I try to engage new people in conversation. I ask about what they do and some are delighted to share their stories as long as the questions are not too invasive. Many do not like this approach, but some are willing to share.

My advice is not to be too pushy, to wait until they are ready to talk, to have patience and to be willing to take no for an answer. It is interesting to talk with people, on its own a benefit, and I have had some great conversations, including some that have led to invitations to special events that ultimately translated to business.

Summary

Developing a network action plan requires a strategy, an energizing attitude and KPIs to achieve your goals. Developing the right strategy involves knowing your objectives, understanding your environment, analyzing your current network – both inside and outside your organization – and identifying how your network needs to be adjusted in line with your goals. Once you have charted your network and identified what can be enhanced, define a plan for which new people to meet and how, or for the best way to strengthen existing relationships. Set specific goals for yourself to make sure you follow through and achieve your objectives.

Questions for consideration

- *What is the structure of your external network?* Are the types of people in it aligned with your objectives? Is its structure aligned with your industry or country environment? Where could you enhance it to achieve better results?

- *What is the structure of your internal organization network?* What is your role: central connector, boundary spanner, information broker or peripheral specialist? Where would you like to enhance your network to improve your ability to facilitate change?

- *What is your networking plan?* How would you like to change your network to align with your objectives? What specific actions can you take to meet new people or build deeper relationships with those you already know? How can you do this in an energizing way? What KPIs can you put in place to be sure that you are consistent in your network building activities to increase the likelihood of achieving your goals?

Ready for implementation

Congratulations. You now understand more about the art and the science of networking and how it applies in different situations. You also know more about how different activities can help you to achieve your objectives and you have your networking plan.

Now your challenge is to put your plan in place!

Remember, anyone can learn to build an effective network. Think about your meaningful purpose, and you will be motivated to action. You don't have to do everything the first week. You may want to take it in steps and identify a quarterly action plan and "rocks" to help you focus and progress in each quarter. Enhancing your approach and your comfort with networking takes time, so consider this a growth experience.

If you want to go into more depth on any of the ideas, the references are included in the back. The authors are some of the best in the networking field and most of the articles are easily accessible so I encourage you to read them and learn more.

Remember that networking is more about coffee and less about cocktails. More about developing relationships and less about exchanging business cards. It takes discipline and effort. People are often happy to help if you approach them in the right way, and remember the magic of serendipity. Be aware of your goals, get yourself out there, and see what magic you can create.

Good luck!

References

[1] https://www.collinsdictionary.com/dictionary/english/networking

[2] https://www.merriam-webster.com/dictionary/networking

[3] https://dictionary.cambridge.org/dictionary/english/networking

[4] http://www.businessdictionary.com/definition/networking.html

[5] Tempest, Nicole and Kathleen McGinn (2000) Heidi Roizen, *Harvard Business School Case Study 9-800-228.*

[6] Uzzi, Brian and Shannon Dunlap (2005) How to build your network, *Harvard Business Review*, December: 53-60.

[7] Cross, Rob, Wayne Baker and Andrew Parker (2003) What creates energy in organizations, *MIT Sloan Management Review*, Summer: 51-56.

[8] Ibid.

[9] Grant, Adam (2013) *Give and Take*, London: Orion Books, Ltd.

[10] Baker, Wayne (2016) Creating a giver culture – tools for action, *Connected Commons Webinar Series.*

[11] www.giveandtake.com.

[12] Anand, N. and Jay Conger (2007) Capabilities of the consummate networker, *Organizational Dynamics*, 36(1): 13-27.

[13] Ibid.

[14] Hall, Jeffrey (2018) How many hours does it take to make a friend? *Journal of Social and Personal Relationships*, March: 1-19.

[15] Wasserman, Stanley and Katherine Faust (1994) *Social Network Analysis*, Cambridge, UK: Cambridge University Press.

[16] Shaner, Janet and Martha Maznevski (2011) The relationship between networks, institutional development and performance in foreign investments, *Strategic Management Journal,* 32: 556-568.

[17] Baum, Joel, Tony Calabrese and Brian Silverman (2000) Don't go it alone: Alliance network composition and startups' performance in Canadian biotechnology, *Strategic Management Journal*, 21: 267-294.

[18] Lee, Choonwoo, Kyungmook Lee and Johannes Pennings (2001) Internal capabilities, external networks and performance: A study on technology-based ventures, *Strategic Management Journal*, 22: 615-640.

[19] Podolny, Joel and J.N. Baron (1997) Resources and relationships: Social networks and mobility in the workplace, *American Sociological Review*, 62 (October): 673-693.

[20] Hall, ibid.

[21] Granovetter, Mark (1973) The strength of weak ties, *American Journal of Sociology*, 78 (May): 1360-1380.

[22] Coleman, James (1988) Social capital in the creation of human capital, *American Journal of Sociology*, 94(Supplement): S95-S120.

[23] Burt, Ron (1998) The gender of social capital, *Rationality and Society*, 10(1): 5-46. Reprinted by permission of SAGE Publications, Ltd.

[24] Uzzi, Brian (1999) Embeddedness in the making of financial capital: How social relations and networks benefit firms seeking financing, *American Sociological Review*, 64 (August): 481-505.

[25] Hansen, Morten (1999) The search-transfer problem: The role of weak ties in sharing knowledge across organization subunits, *Administrative Science Quarterly*, 44: 82-111.

[26] Rowley, Tim, Dean Behrens and David Krackhardt (2000) Redundant governance structures: An analysis of structural and relational embeddedness in the steel and semiconductor industries, *Strategic Management Journal*, 21: 369-386.

[27] Kadushin, Charles (2002) The motivational foundations of social networks, *Social Networks*, 24: 77-91.

[28] Shaner, Janet and Martha Maznevski (2006) Building the right networks for business performance, *IMD Perspectives for Managers*, No. 132, March.

[29] Xin, Katherine and Jone Pearce (1996) *Guanxi*: Connections as substitutes for formal institutional support, *Academy of Management Journal*, 39(6): 1641-1658.

[30] Shaner, Janet, Jim Pulcrano and William Fischer (2007) Networking across cultures: Different cultures demand different networks, in *Anticipating the Future*, Lausanne: IMD, 181-189.

[31] Ibid.

[32] Burt, ibid.

[33] Uzzi, ibid.

[34] Pentland, Alex "Sandy" (2013) Beyond the echo chamber, *Harvard Business Review*, November: 80-86.

[35] Perry-Smith, Jill and Pier Vittorio Mannucci (2017) From creativity to innovation: Drivers of the four phases of the idea journey, *Academy of Management Review*, 42(1): 53-79. Republished with permission of the Academy of Management; permission conveyed through Copyright Clearance Center, Inc.

[36] Hassin, Bryan (2018) http://greenknig.ht/2018/03/startup-fundraising-good-bad-and-ugly.html

[37] Baum, Calabrese and Silverman, ibid.

[38] Lee, Lee and Pennings, ibid.

[39] Milanov Hana and Dean Shepert (2013) The importance of first relationship: The ongoing influence of initial network on future status, *Strategic Management Journal*, 34: 727-750.

[40] Burt, ibid.

[41] Ibarra, Herminia (1992) Homophily and differential returns: Sex differences in network structure and access in an advertising firm, *Administrative Science Quarterly*, 37: 422-447.

[42] Ibarra, Herminia (1995) Race, opportunity and diversity of social circles in managerial networks, *Academy of Management Journal*, 38(3): 673-703.

[43] Konrad, Alison, Vaughan Radcliffe and Duckjung Shin (2016) Participation in helping networks as social capital mobilization: Impact on influence for domestic men, domestic women and international students, *Academy of Management Learning and Development*, 15(1): 60-78.

[44] https://medtechwomen.org/

[45] Porot, Daniel. https://www.porot.com

[46] Granovetter, ibid.

[47] Bolles, Richard (2018) *What Color Is Your Parachute?*, New York, NY: Ten Speed Press.

[48] Grant, ibid.

[49] Porot, ibid.

[50] Shaner, Janet (2018) Career networking workshop, Ecole hôtelière de Lausanne (EHL).

[51] Krackhardt, David and Jeffrey Hanson (1993) Informal networks: The company, *Harvard Business Review,* July-August: 104-111.

[52] Cross, Rob and Laurence Prusak (2002) The people who make organizations Go – or Stop, *Harvard Business Review*, June: 104-112.

[53] Cross, Rob, Stephen Borgatti and Andrew Parker (2002) Making invisible work visible, *California Management Review*, 44(2): 25-46. Reprinted by permission of SAGE Publications, Inc.

[54] Ibid.

[55] Liedtka, Jeanne (2016) *Creating the innovative workplace*, University of Virginia, Darden School Foundation

[56] Battilana, Julie and Tiziana Casciaro (2013) Network secrets of great change agents, *Harvard Business Review*, July-August: 62-68.

[57] Vissa, Balagopal and Aya Chacar (2009) Leveraging ties: The contingent value of entrepreneurial teams' external advice networks on Indian software venture performance, *Strategic Management Journal*, 30: 1179-1191.

[58] Moran, Peter (2005) Structural vs. relational embeddedness: Social capital and managerial performance, *Strategic Management Journal*, 26:1129-1151.

[59] Capaldo, Antonio (2007) Network structure and innovation: The leveraging of a dual network as a distinctive relational capability, *Strategic Management Journal*, 28: 585-608.

[60] Carnabuci Gianluca and Bálint Diószegi (2015) Social networks, cognitive style and innovative performance: A contingency perspective, *Academy of Management Journal*, 58(3): 881-905.

[61] Bartlett, Christopher (2000) McKinsey and Company: Managing knowledge and learning, *Harvard Business School Case Study 9-396-357.*

[62] Port, Michael (2017) *Book Yourself Solid*, Hoboken, NJ: John Wiley and Sons, Inc.

[63] The use of 92 (ninety-two) words from PRESENCE: HOW TO USE POSITIVE ENERGY FOR SUCCESS IN EVERY SITUATION written by Patsy Rodenburg and published by Penguin Books, 2009. First published by Michael Joseph, 2007. Copyright © Patsy Rodenburg, 2007. Reproduced by permission of Penguin Books Ltd.

[64] Barrat, Christopher (2019) Networking: 10 tips for success.

[65] Young, Kirsty (2011) Social ties, social networks and the Facebook experience, *International Journal of Emerging Technologies and Society*, 9(1): 20-34.

[66] Jairing, Païvi and Asta Bäck (2017) How researchers use social media to promote their research and network with industry, *Technology Innovation Management Review*, 7(8): 32-39.

[67] Dietel, Jana-Eva (2017) They do! How the explicit motive-structure predicts user behavior in (business) social network sites like Xing or LinkedIn, *Computing*, 99: 537-550.

[68] Borgatti, S.P., M.G. Everett and L.C. Freeman (2002) UCINET for Windows: Software for social network analysis. Harvard, MA: Analytic Technologies.

[69] Shaner and Maznevski, ibid.

[70] Cross, Baker and Parker, ibid.

About the author

Dr. Janet Shaner is an expert in learning, networking and managing organizations, as well as an experienced workshop facilitator and writer.

She has 20+ years' experience in the management education industry, including program management and marketing for MBA and Executive MBA programs at IMD business school and INSEAD. She has developed award-winning case studies and class exercises with IMD and Harvard Business School. Her industry experience includes seven years in product marketing and sponsorship with Champion Athletic Apparel, including a role as Director of Olympic Marketing.

Janet is a networking expert both through academic research and in real-world practice. She earned her doctorate at the University of Lausanne, researching the relationship between external business networks and performance in foreign investments. She holds a BBA in Finance from the University of Iowa and an MBA from Harvard Business School.

As an entrepreneur, Janet is President of Top10 Learning Solutions. Services related to networking include workshops for careers, entrepreneurs and organizations, as well as individual coaching and guidance on designing activities for more effective networking.

www.top10learningsolutions.com

www.ingramcontent.com/pod-product-compliance
Lightning Source LLC
Chambersburg PA
CBHW030840180526
45163CB00004B/1396